*A Montgomery
Chicago 1980*

TRANSCRIPTION AND TRANSLITERATION

An annotated bibliography
on Conversion of Scripts

by

Hans (Hanan) Wellisch

Institute of Modern Languages
Silver Spring, Maryland

© 1975 by Institute of Modern Languages
All rights reserved

No part of this book may be reproduced
in any form without the permission of
Institute of Modern Languages.

Published by
Institute of Modern Languages
Publishers in the Languages of the World
2622-24 Pittman Drive
Silver Spring, Maryland 20910

Library of Congress Catalog Card Number 74-77274
ISBN 0-88499-149-0
Printed in the United States of America

CONTENTS

Arrangement of entries v

Introduction ix

List of sources xvii
   i) Periodicals xvii
  ii) *Festschriften* xxiii
 iii) Conference proceedings and other collective works xxiv

Bibliography on transcription and transliteration 1

Addenda 103

Author and title index 107

Subject index 121

ARRANGEMENT OF ENTRIES

Entries in the first section GENERALITIES (Scripts, Transliteration and transcription in general, Bibliographical and library work, Catalog codes and rules, Re-transliteration) are arranged chronologically. All following entries are generally arranged by source language or script, following the scheme used in the Linguistic Bibliography as displayed in its Table of contents for the year 1969. The target languages or scripts are also arranged in the same manner. Where more than one entry is about the same source and target language or script, the entries are arranged first chronologically, then alphabetically by author's name.

The titles of some sources are abbreviated in accordance with ANSI Z 39.5, Standard for the Abbreviation of Titles of Periodicals. Festschriften are indicated by [Festschr. ...] followed by the name of the person honored. Titles of conference proceedings and collective works are followed by [C]. Full bibliographical data for all sources will be found in the List of Sources on p. xvii.

I. GENERALITIES 1

    Scripts 1
    Transliteration and transcription (general) 5
    Bibliographical and library work 8
    Catalog codes and rules 11
    Re-transliteration 14

II. INDO-EUROPEAN LANGUAGES 14

    Indo-Aryan languages 14
        Sanskrit 14
        Modern Indic languages 15
        Kurdish 19
        Iranian (Persian) 19
        Pushto 20

    Armenian 20
    Albanian 21
    Greek 21
    Latin 23
    Romance languages 24
        Spanish 24
        Ladino 24
        Judeo-Arabic 24
        Portuguese 25
        French 25
        Italian 25
        Romanian 25
    Gaelic 26

       <u>Germanic languages</u> 26
- German 26
- Yiddish 27
- Dutch 28
- English 28
- Danish 29
- Swedish 29

<u>Baltic languages</u> 29
- Lithuanian 29

<u>Slavic languages</u> 29
- Church Slavic 38
- Bulgarian 38
- Macedonian 39
- Serbo-Croatian 39
- Slovenian 39
- Czech 39
- Slovakian 40
- Polish 41
- Russian 41
- Ukrainian 51
- White-Russian 52

III. ORIENTAL LANGUAGES 55

IV. HAMITO-SEMITIC LANGUAGES 58

- Hebrew 59
- Arabic 64
- Judeo-Arabic 70
- Amharic 70
- Coptic 70

V. CAUCASIAN LANGUAGES 71

- Georgian 71

VI. LANGUAGES OF EURASIA AND NORTHERN ASIA 71

<u>Uralian languages</u> 71
- Finnish 71
- Hungarian 71

<u>Altaic languages</u> 72
- Turkish (Osmanli) 72
- Other Turkic languages 73
- Mongolian 75
- Tungus-Manchu 75

<u>Korean</u> 75
<u>Japanese</u> 76

VII. DRAVIDIAN LANGUAGES 80

      Kannada 80
      Tamil 80
      Malayalam 80
      Telugu 81

VIII. LANGUAGES OF SOUTH-EAST ASIA 81

      Sino-Tibetan languages 81
         Chinese 81
         Tibetan 92
         Thai 92
      Vietnamese 94
      Cambodian 94

IX. LANGUAGES OF NEGRO AFRICA 94

X. AMERICAN LANGUAGES 95

XI. GYPSY LANGUAGES 95

XII. TRANSLITERATION AND TRANSCRIPTION OF PLACE NAMES 96

INTRODUCTION

This bibliography is an attempt to bring together the widely-scattered literature on a subject which has long been the cinderella of the library world and of bibliographical control in general: the conversion of one script into another. The subject has, however, now assumed a growing importance due to the steadily growing flow of literature written in non-Roman scripts, some of which comes from countries which only recently became producers of literature. It is further accented by the growth of libraries serving a multi-lingual community which in many cases is also, at the same time, a multi-script community. The methods used hitherto seem to be inadequate to cope with these phenomena, but in order to understand the problems in all their multi-faceted aspects, it is necessary to survey the field and to take stock of what has been achieved so far and which of the many difficulties have yet to be solved.

With this aim in mind, I made an effort to list as many items as I could find when conducting an extensive literature search on the topics of transliteration and transcription from and into any script. I did not try to make a selection on the basis of scholarly level or quality: the reader will find here both the good, the bad and the indifferent, and indeed sometimes the outright silly. The reason for this catholic approach is twofold: firstly, this seems to be the first bibliography of the subject and in such a first attempt nothing should be excluded in order to give as comprehensive a picture as possible; secondly, future writers on the subject who may hopefully use the present compilation before embarking upon their own endeavours, may find useful hints in even the more abstruse or popular writings on the subject.

Scope

The criterion for inclusion of an item was that at least one of the languages or scripts dealt with is spoken or used today. Thus, items about the transcription of ancient tongues such as Sumeric or Egyptian have not been included (which explains why there are no entries on the Rosetta stone and similar monuments), but an item on, say, a transcription from Sanskrit into Chinese does qualify for inclusion since Chinese is spoken and used today. Excluded also is the voluminous literature on purely phonetic transcription of one language or general treatises on this subject, except for the historically important works of Lepsius and the proposals of the Copenhagen conference of 1925 and commentaries on these. Newspaper articles and very short notes on the subject in periodicals have also been excluded.

One of the more astonishing aspects brought to light by this bibliography is the fact that the subject of transliteration and transcription does not have a "core" of principal journals in which contributions are published. The overwhelming majority of entries come from journals which published a contribution on the topic but once, and only a few journals contributed two or more items. This means that researchers on this subject cannot keep abreast of developments by scanning a few outstanding journals or even by routinely checking the current bibliographies such as the <u>Linguistic Bibliography</u> or the <u>MLA International Bibliography</u> (both of which were used in the compilation of this bibliography but yielded comparatively few entries).

Terminology

Following the established usage of ISO, the term "Transliteration" is employed for "representing the characters (letters or signs) of one alphabet by those of another, in principle letter by letter", whereas "Transcription" is used for "the operation of representing the elements of a language, either sounds or signs, however they may be written originally, in any other written system of letters or sound signs." When both systems are involved, and for general discussions of the whole topic, the term "Romanization" (also following ISO and the Library of Congress) is used, although it is limited to conversion into a particular script and lacks the universality of the German term "Umschrift" which has no equivalent in English. Conversion into other scripts is consequently termed Arabization, Cyrillization or Hebraization, as the case may be. For conversion into other scripts, no such "-ization" terms seem to exist. I have used the phrase "Transcription into...".

My usage of "Latinization", however, needs explanation. The basic connotations of this term are (i) the rendering of a non-Latin name in a form which resembles Latin (such as Guilelmus Turnerus for William Turner) or its translation into Latin (such as Avienus for Vogel); (ii) the transliteration into Roman characters of any other script. In French, there is indeed no such term as "Romanization"; "latinisation" is always used to express transcription into the Roman alphabet. Some English writers on the subject have also used the term Latinisation in this sense. But since the term "Romanization" has now gained official recognition, I have used "Latinization" for the complete and official conversion of a country's or a nation's script to Roman characters <u>by decree</u>, as distinct from Romanization schemes used for philological or bibliographical purposes. Examples are the Latinization of the Turkish language in 1928 and the movement for Latinization of Russian and the scripts of non-Slavic peoples in the Soviet Union. The latter was advocated by Lenin and gained momentum in the early 30'ies but became one of the victims of Stalin's ideas on language and its role in society and politics; the trend towards Latinisation was abruptly halted in 1937, all Latinized alphabets of various Soviet nations were summarily scrapped, and the Cyrillic alphabet substituted. At least one American writer on the subject (see no. 505) has used the term "Latinisation" in the sense of official Romanization, so that there is some precedent for it. The attempts to Romanize the Chinese and Japanese script, however, have not been subsumed under the heading "Latinization". Although, in the case of Chinese, such a movement has had the official sanction of the government, the introduction of Roman characters was not intended to supplant the use of the traditional Chinese ideograms (which latter have also undergone a process of "simplification" under the Communist regime) but only to serve as a kind of parallel script. In the case of Japanese, the movement for Romanization is not an official one, and no wholesale "Latinization" of the Japanese script by decree is envisaged for the foreseeable future.

For the English names of languages, the terminology of the <u>Linguistic Bibliography</u> has generally been followed. This will explain the use of "Slavic" instead of "Slavonic", although some linguists maintain that the latter is the only appropriate term in English and the issue has been hotly debated in professional journals. Following the same source, the term "Byelo-Russian" has been avoided and the language in question is named "White-Russian". The name "Byelo-Russian" is a quaint hybrid, composed of one Russian and one English element which do not give a clue to the reader unfamiliar with Russian that the first is simply an adjective defining the latter. Incongruously, the ISO/R9 transliteration standard[*] lists this language in a column-head as "Byelo-Russian" when according to its own rules it would have to be transliterated as "Belo-Russian", if indeed this name is used at all.

<u>Scripts</u>

Although the topic of script as such is intrinsic to the subject of this bibliography, it would have been beyond its scope to include even a selection of relevant references.[**] The entries presented under this heading in the first section were chosen with respect to their bearing on the main subject, e.g. attempts at the creation of some "universal alphabet" (inevitably based on Roman characters) in which "all" languages could be written, or other writings in which the topic of script has been linked expressly to Romanization. Some entries dealing with diacritical marks have also been included because of the importance of these in Romanization schemes in general, and more particular in the perennial debate whether or not Romanization for English-speaking readers should make use of diacritics.

<u>Transliteration</u>

Names in non-Roman characters have been transliterated according to the appropriate ISO standards. In the case of Cyrillic, the basic ISO scheme has been followed, i.e. the one using diacritical marks. Since the bibliography is written in English and is intended mainly for English-speaking readers, it would seem, on the face of it, that the "Anglo-Saxon" alternative now permitted by ISO/R9 should have been used. However, when citing names in other Slavic languages using the

---

[*] Until 1971, ISO issued "Recommendations" which could be adopted by member states as their "standards" in the same or in modified form. Since 1972, ISO's publications are called "Standards".

[**] One of the most comprehensive bibliographies on scripts may be found in Diringer's work <u>The Alphabet</u> (see item 63).

Roman alphabet, diacritical marks had to be used anyway and the use of
the basic ISO scheme makes the rendering of Slavic names more uniform.
In addition, the use of certain digraphs such as ch in the "Anglo-
Saxon" version of ISO/R9 when used in conjunction with ISO standards
for other scripts may lead to ambiguities which are largely avoided
when the version with diacritical marks is used. The fact that international agencies such as Unesco or INIS are firmly committed to the
basic ISO transliteration of Cyrillic is a further reason for its use
in this bibliography since it is always desirable to be in conformity
with accepted international standard practice.

Arrangement of entries

It is not easy to decide on the mode of arrangement in a bibliography of this kind, where so many entries are related in more than one
way to others, and where the interests of different groups of users
have to be kept in mind. There are probably as many people interested
in a particular language and the conversion of its script into other
scripts, as there are people who wish to look at a particular script
and to investigate the ways in which it has been used or adapted to
the needs of a particular language. This means that the main arrangement of the bibliography could be made by language (which disperses the
entries on a particular script) or by script (which conversely disperses the entries on languages).

I decided, after consultation with linguists and bibliographers,
to follow the first alternative, i.e. grouping by language, following
the arrangement of the Linguistic Bibliography, the most general and
internationally oriented bibliographic tool in this subject area.
Those users primarily interested in a particular script will find all
relevant entries in the Subject index. The cross references given
after each language section should also be useful in this respect.
Under each heading, the subarrangement is chronological which, I hope,
will serve the purpose of showing the development of certain trends.
Examples are the interest in better transliteration of Russian in East
Germany after the war (caused by the heavy dependence on Soviet literature in this country, first under the Soviet occupation and later
as one of the "People's democracies" or satellites of the Soviet Union);
in the late 50'ies, another trend can be discerned in the growing
Soviet literature on Cyrillization of foreign languages and scripts,
probably one of the consequences of the partial "thaw" after Stalin's
death which made scientific treatment of social and cultural topics
from outside the Soviet Union no longer politically suspect and dan-
gerous. In another sphere, it can be seen how religious and missionary
motives for the Romanization of Indic languages gradually gave way to
more worldly reasons, and so on.

Some entries have been listed twice. This was done when one
entry dealt with two languages or scripts which, due to the linguistic
plan of arrangement, are widely separated from each other in the
bibliography. Few people will read a bibliography of this kind from
cover to cover, and I thought it best to provide direct access by

double entries, e.g. for Arabic and Persian where these are discussed in one article. The size of the bibliography is not much enlarged by doing so, but the convenience to the reader should be considerable.

The numbering of entries is in some instances not quite consistent: there are numbers with an a, and on the other hand, a few numbers are missing from the sequence. This is due to last-minute re-arrangements of entries as well as to the fact that I found additional entries after the main task of editing and cross-referencing had been completed. I hope that readers will not be disturbed by this minor blemish, for which I take the full blame.

"See also" references to other relevant entries are always concentrated at the end of a section (which is clearly marked by the device of ***) printed beneath the last entry. Thus, the cross-references do not relate to the last entry only but to the whole section devoted to a language or script. References to transliterations and transcriptions from other languages or scripts into the one dealt with in a section are given in the systematic order in which they appear in the bibliography, in order to keep references to related languages together. However, the subject index lists these language or script pairs also in alphabetical order.

Romanization

Under "Romanization" all entries dealing with conversion of the script of a source language in general, (i.e. using the Roman alphabet without regard to any particular target language) have been listed; for practical reasons, all entries dealing with transliteration or transcription into the English language have also been listed under the same heading, because they form the majority of entries on any script, and it is in many cases not possible to separate the arguments on the Romanization of a script in general from its adaptation mainly or exclusively for English readers. But wherever Romanization of a script is treated with respect to the special requirements of a target language other than English, the entries have been arranged under the respective languages.

Cyrillization

A similar arrangement applies to the sections on "Cyrillization" where of course the majority of entries deals with conversion of a script for Russian readers, but some are devoted to the requirements of Bulgarian. The entries in the section "Cyrillization" following the Slavic languages (p. 52-54) deal only with general problems or with Cyrillization from many languages; entries on Cyrillization of individual languages and scripts will be found under the relevant language because I thought it more important to keep all entries on transcription and transliteration of any one language or script together. Cross references to these entries are provided at the end of the general Cyrillization section and in the Subject index.

Slavic languages

The entries on Slavic languages, the Cyrillic script and Russian posed special problems of arrangement. I decided to keep all entries on Cyrillic script together in one group, i.e. those which deal with either the script as such or with more than one language written in that script, and its transliteration into Roman (subdivided by language). Then follow the individual Slavic languages and their Romanization where under Russian will be found those entries dealing only with the Romanization of that language.

Oriental languages

This section has been included although it has strictly no basis in linguistics since a number of entries deal in a general way with "Oriental" languages, or discuss several Asian vernaculars which fall into different language groups. I thought it best not to split up these entries or to repeat them under each relevant language. Cross-references are, of course, provided.

Place names

The transliteration and transcription of place names has produced such a large body of literature and is of such importance nationally as well as internationally, that a special section of the bibliography has been devoted to it. Where an entry deals with personal names or other topics as well as place names, it has generally been listed under the relevant language or script, with cross references provided at the end of the section on place names.

Romanization systems of encyclopedias

The systems of Romanization used by large encyclopedias devoted specially to Jewish or Islamic topics were scanned for inclusion in the bibliography, because one would expect that these would give special attention to Hebrew and Arabic script. The Jewish encyclopedias display specific Romanization systems for Hebrew (and most of them have also schemes for the Romanization of Arabic and Cyrillic script). The first edition of the Encyclopedia of Islam (1911-1938), however, had neither a table of Romanization for Arabic script, nor did it contain an entry for Transliteration, despite the fact that a large body of literature on the subject existed. The second edition (1954-) displays a Romanization system for Arabic and Cyrillic script only in its second volume (reprinted in each subsequent volume); it has not yet reached the letter T, so that it is not known at present whether the subject of transliteration will be treated this time. The Index Islamicus (1958-), although in other respects an excellent and scholarly work of reference, omits any hint to which transliteration system is used.

The general encyclopedias of the Western world display tables of transliteration for most non-Roman scripts, and some also have more or less extensive entries on the subject. The Soviet Bol'šaja Enciklopedija, on the other hand, gives no clue as to which system it follows in transcribing names and words from other languages, and its entry on Transliteration deals only with the phonetic alphabet and its use for linguistic purposes, with examples from Russian.

Translation of titles

All titles in languages other than English have been translated into English* because this bibliography is intended not only for the use of linguists (who presumably have at least some basic knowledge of the major languages) but also for bibliographers and librarians, most of which are unfortunately not as conversant with foreign languages as their profession would seem to demand. Complete translation of all titles in a language other than the one in which the bibliography is presented also avoids quarrelsome disputes over what constitutes a "major" or a "well-known" language from which apparently no translation is needed. This partial approach to translation of titles in a bibliography has always seemed snobbish to me, because it implies that whatever the editor or compiler can translate for himself should "obviously" be known to the users of his bibliography, whereas other languages are deemed to be "obscure". The other extreme, not to translate anything, deprives probably most readers of such a bibliography of the meaningful use of a majority of the entries. If this is so for titles in Roman characters (where at least some hints in the form of Latin or Greek roots are sometimes discernible, and dictionaries can be used) it applies even more to transliterated or transcribed titles not followed by a translation. For anyone not familiar with the source language, the Romanization of a discursive title (as opposed to the Romanization of a proper name or family name) is virtually meaningless and constitutes no more than an unintelligible string of nonsense syllables, most of which do not even lend themselves to pronunciation (at least not to someone who does not know the language involved). Conversely, for the reader who is familiar with the source language and its script, a transliteration is more of a hindrance than an aid, and he does not need it anyway.

Entries in scripts other than the Roman alphabet have therefore been given only in translation followed by an indication of the original language. Inasmuch as the title of an entry reveals the subject matter dealt with (and most of the translated titles in this collection are quite indicative) the reader is much better served than with a more or less faithful rendering of the sounds of a foreign language in the form of entirely unintelligible strings of characters to which no dictionary can give any clue. In the case of logographic scripts such as Chinese and Japanese, the so-called transcription of titles by whichever system is completely meaningless even for Chinese or Japanese readers who have to see the original characters in order to be able to understand the meaning. In the few instances where Romanized Chinese has been used in an entry, the Romanization appears in the document itself in this form.

---

*Except those which were originally published in one or more translations, e.g. items 36-38.

Abbreviations of titles

In the interest of clarity and easier reference, most titles of periodicals have generally been given in full. Long titles, particularly those which are cited more frequently, have been abbreviated according to ANSI standard Z 39.5-1969 Abbreviation of titles of periodicals.

Annotations

Annotations have been provided for entries which are of particular importance, for many of those which are in foreign languages and when titles are not fully descriptive of the subject content. Many annotations also serve as links between related items. I tried to inspect as many of the entries as possible, but some had to be taken from other sources without a possibility to check them for accuracy and actual scope. These, however, constitute only a small part of the bibliography.

* * *

It is my hope that this bibliography will serve to highlight the fact that conversion of scripts is not a one-way street: though Romanization has historically dominated the efforts to make the world's literature written in scripts other than the Roman accessible for those who do not know those scripts (at least so far as the names of authors and titles are concerned), the nations using non-Roman scripts also have to tackle the problem of rendering names and titles in Western languages into their writing systems.

There is also clearly a need for better transcription schemes and more standardization in their application, particularly in the fields of bibliographic control and cartography. But Romanization, Cyrillization, etc. of names and words alone will probably not provide effective means of control of documents in differing scripts, as the number of such documents emanating from many countries which formerly produced little or no literature in the vernacular is steadily increasing. Bibliographic control may have to rely on numerical codes (possibly used in conjunction with transcribed renderings of names and titles), since these are best suited for handling of data by machines.

The use of computers has scarcely begun to attract the attention of scholar in this field (there are no more than a handful of references to computers in this bibliography), but it is sure to produce more contributions in the future.

These and other future developments will inevitably have to draw upon the information already available in the literature on conversion of scripts written during the last one hundred years or so. If the present bibliography will become an aid to those future researchers and prevent them from duplicating much of the work that has already been performed (as is so painfully obvious from many of the entries which merely repeat the same old arguments over and over again) it will have served its purpose.

H.W.

LIST OF SOURCES

i) Periodicals

Abgila (Calcutta)
Abhandlungen der Akademie der Wissenschaften, Berlin. (Berlin)
Abhandlungen der Akademie der Wissenschaften, Mainz. Geistes- und
   sozialwissenschaftliche Klasse. (Mainz)
Academia Scientiarum Hungarica, see
   Acta Orient. Acad. Sci. Hung.
   Stud. Slov. Acad. Sci. Hung.
Academy of the Hebrew Language, see Zikhronot ha-aqademya
Accademie e Biblioteche d'Italia (Firenze)
Acta Orientalia Academiae Scientiarum Hungaricae (Budapest)
Adyar Library Bulletin (Madras)
Akademija Nauk Latvijskoj S.S.R., see Izv. Akad. Nauk Latv.
Akademija Nauk S.S.R., see
   Izv. Akad. Nauk S.S.R., Otd. Lit. Jaz.
   Izv. Akad. Nauk S.S.R., Ser. Geogr.
   Trudy Akad. Nauk S.S.R., Sibirsk. Otd.
Akademija Nauk (Sanktpeterburg), see
   Izv. Otd. Russk. Jaz. Imp. Akad. Nauk
Aktualne Problemy Informacji i Dokumentacji (Warszawa)
'Alam al-Maktabat (Cairo)
American Association of Teachers of Slavic and East European Languages
   (AATSEEL), see Bull. AATSEEL
American Documentation (Washington, D.C.)
American Journal of Semitic Languages and Literature (Chicago)
American Journal of Sociology (Chicago)
American Oriental Society, see J. Amer. Orient. Soc.
American Schools of Oriental Research, see Bull. Amer. Sch. Orient. Res
American Slavic and East European Review (Menasha, Wis.)
American Society for Information Science, see
   J. Amer. Soc. Inform. Sci.
Arbeitsblätter für betriebliches Informationswesen (Frankfurt/Main)
Archeion (Roma)
Archiv für Schreib- und Buchwesen (Wolfenbüttel)
Asia Major (Leipzig)
Asian Affairs (London)
Asiatic Society of Japan Transactions (Yokohama)
Asiatick Researches (Calcutta)
Asiatische Forschungen (Wiesbaden)
Associação Brasileira de Normas Técnicas, see
   Bol. Ass. Brasil. Norm. Tec.
Babel (Bonn)
Bǎlgarski Ezik (Sofia)
Bantu Studies (Johannesburg)
Die Bergakademie (Berlin)
Bibliografijos Žinios (Kaunas)
Bibliotheca Orientalis (Leiden)
Bibliotheeksgids (Antwerpen)
Bibliotheekleven (Rotterdam)
Bibliothekar (Leipzig)
Bibliothèque Nationale, see Notic. Extr. Manuscr. Bibl. Nat.
Biuletyn Fonograficzny (Poznań)

Boletim da Associação Brasileira de Normas Técnicas (Rio de Janeiro)
Boletin de Bibliotecas y de Bibliografia (Madrid)
Books Abroad (Norman, Okla.)
Börsenblatt für den deutschen Buchhandel (Leipzig)
British Academy, see Proc. Brit. Acad.
Bulletin AATSEEL (New York)
Bulletin de la Société de Linguistique de Paris (Paris)
Bulletin de l'Ecole Française d'Extrême-Orient (Hanoi)
Bulletin de l'Institut Français d'Afrique Noire (Paris)
Bulletin de l'Institut Français d'Archéologie Orientale (Cairo)
Bulletin des Bibliothèques de France (Paris)
Bulletin des Relations Scientifiques (Paris)
Bulletin Hispanique (Bordeaux)
Bulletin Mensuel du Comité de l'Asie Française (Paris)
Bulletin of the American Schools of Oriental Research (New Haven, Conn.)
Bulletin of the Faculty of Arts. Cairo University (Cairo)
Bulletin of the Medical Library Association (Baltimore)
Bulletin of the School of Oriental and African Studies (London)
Burma Research Society, see J. Burma Res. Soc.
Cahiers du Monde Russe et Soviétique (Paris)
Cairo University. Faculty of Arts, see Bull. Fac. Arts, Cairo Univ.
Canadian Library Association Bulletin (Ottawa)
Časopis pro Moderni Filologii (Praha)
Cataloging Service (Washington, D.C.)
Catholic church in China. Synodal commission, see
    Collectanea Commissionis Synodalis
Ceylon Literary Register (Colombo)
Chinese Social and Political Science Review (Peking)
Chung-kuo yu-wen (Peking)
Collectanea Commissionis Synodalis (Peiping)
College and Research Libraries (Chicago)
Comité de l'Afrique Française, see Renseign. Colon.
Comité de l'Asie Française, see Bull. mens. Comit. Asie Franc.
Comptes Rendus du Groupe Linguistique d'Etudes Chamito-Semitiques (Bordeaux)
Correspondence d'Orient Politique, Economique et Financière (Paris)
Courier de la Normalisation (Paris)
Czasopismo Geograficzne (Łodz)
Deutsche Akademie der Wissenschaften zu Berlin, see
    Mitt. Inst. Orientforsch.
Deutsche Morgenländische Gesellschaft, see
    Z. Deut. Morgenl. Ges.
DIN-Mitteilungen (Berlin)
La Documentation en France (Paris)
Dokumentation (Leipzig)
Dokumentation, Fachbibliothek, Werksbücherei (Hannover)
Dokumentation und Arbeitstechnik (Berlin)
Ecole Française d'Extrême Orient, see
    Bull. Ecole Franc. Extr. Orient
Ecole Nationale des Langues Orientales, see
    Rev. Ecol. Nat. Lang. Orient.
Epigrafika Vostoka (Moskva)

Estudios Geograficos (Madrid)
Etudes Tsiganes (Paris)
L'Europa Orientale (Roma)
Fédération Internationale de Documentation, see
    Trans. Int. Fed. Docum.
Filología Moderna (Madrid)
Filologishe shriftn (Vilna)
Forschungen und Fortschritte (Berlin)
Fremdsprachen (Halle/Saale)
Fremdsprachenunterricht (Berlin)
Gdańskie Zeszyty Humanistyczne. 10. Filologia Rosyjska. (Gdańsk)
Geographical Journal (London)
Geographical Review (New York)
Germanisch-romanische Monatsschrift (Heidelberg)
Groupe Linguistique d'Etudes Chamito-Semitiques, see
    Comt. Rend. Groupe Linguist. Etud. Chamito-Semit.
Gutenberg-Jahrbuch (Mainz)
Harvard Journal of Asiatic Studies (Cambridge, Mass.)
Harvard Theological Review (Cambridge, Mass.)
Hebrew Union College Annual (Cincinnati)
Herald of Library Science (Varanasi, India)
Humboldt-Universität zu Berlin, see
    Wiss. Z. Humboldt Univ., Ges. Sprachwiss.
Indian Librarian (Jullundur, India)
Indian Linguistics (Lahore)
Indica (Bombay)
Indogermanische Forschungen (Strasbourg)
Industrial and Engineering Chemistry (Easton, Pa.)
Informatik (Berlin)
Institut Français d'Afrique Noire, see
    Bull. Inst. Franc. Afr. Noire
Institut Français d'Archéologie Orientale, see
    Bull. Inst. Franc. Archeol. Orient.
Institut für Orientforschung, see Mitt. Inst. Orientforsch.
Institut für österreichische Geschichtsforschung, see
    Mitt. Inst. österr. Geschichtsforsch.
International Cataloguing (London)
International Federation of Documentation, see
    Trans. Int. Fed. Docum.
Islamic Culture (Hyderabad)
Izvestija Akademii Nauk Latvijskoj S.S.R. (Riga)
Izvestija Akademii Nauk S.S.S.R. Otdelenie Literatury i Jazyka (Moskva)
Izvestija Akademii Nauk S.S.S.R. Serija Geografičeskaja (Moskva)
Izvestija Otdelenija Russkogo Jazyka i Slovestnosti Imp. Akademii Nauk
    (St. Petersburg)
Izvestija Vsesojuznogo Geografičeskogo Obščestva (Moskva)
Japan Society, see Trans. Proc. Japan Soc.
Język Polski (Kraków)
Journal Asiatique (Paris)
Journal of Chemical Education (Easton, Pa.)
Journal of Documentation (London)
Journal of Near Eastern Studies (Chicago)

Journal of the American Oriental Society (New Haven)
Journal of the American Society for Information Science (Washington, D.C.)
Journal of the Burma Research Society (Rangoon)
Journal of the North China Branch of the Royal Asiatic Society (Shanghai)
Journal of the Regional Cultural Institute (Iran, Pakistan, Turkey) (Tehran)
Journal of the Royal Asiatic Society (London)
Journal of the Thailand Society (Rangoon)
Journal of the Washington Academy of Sciences (Washington, D.C.)
Journal of Theological Studies (London)

Kaiserliche Akademie der Wissenschaften, see
   Sitzungsber. Phil. Hist. Cl., Kaiserl. Akad. Wiss.
Koninklijke Vlaamsche Aacdemie voor Wetenschappen (etc.), see
   Mededel. Kon. Vlaam. Acad. Wetensch.
Kotobano Kyoiki (Tokyo)
Kul'tura i Pis'mennost' Vostoka (Moskva)

Lebende Sprachen (Berlin)
Leningradskij Universitet, see
   Uc. Zap. Ser. Filol. Nauk., Leningr. Univ.
   Vest. Leningr. Univ., Ser. Biol.
Library Association Record (London)
Library Journal (New York)
Library of Congress Information Bulletin (Washington, D.C.)
Library Quarterly (Chicago)
Library Resources and Technical Services (Chicago)
Libri (Copenhagen)
Limba Romînă (Bucureşti)
Lingua (Haarlem)
Listy Filologické (Praha)

Magyar Könyvszemle (Budapest)
Le Maître Phonétique (Paris)
Mededelingen van de Koninklijke Vlaamsche Academie voor Wetenschappen,
   Letteren en Schone Kunsten van Belgie. Klasse der Letteren. (Brüssel)
Medical Library Association, see Bull. Med. Libr. Ass.
Memoires de la Société de Linguistique de Paris (Paris)
Mitteilungen des Instituts für Orientforschung. Deutsche Akademie der
   Wissenschaften zu Berlin. (Berlin)
Mitteilungen des Instituts für österreichische Geschichtsforschung (Wien)
Mitteilungen des Seminars für orientalische Sprachen zu Berlin. (Berlin)
Monde Oriental (Uppsala)
The Music Student (Leeds)
Musical Times (London)

Nachrichten aus dem Reichsvermessungsdienst (Berlin)
Nachrichten für Dokumentation (Frankfurt/Main)
Narody Azii i Afriki (Moskva)
Nature (London)
Naučne Trudy Taškentskogo Gosudarstvennogo Universiteta im. V.I. Lenina.
   Filologičeskie Nauki. (Taškent)
Naučno-tehničeskaja Informacija (Moskva)
Die Neue Gesellschaft (Berlin)

Neuvostoliittoinstituuti. Vuosikirja (Helsinki)
New Englander and Yale Review (New Haven, Conn.)
Nippon (Tokyo)
Nordisk Tidskrift för Bok- och Biblioteksväsen (Uppsala)
Normalizacja (Warszawa)
Notices et Extraits des Manuscrits de la Bibliothèque Nationale (Paris)

Orbis (Louvain)
Oriens (Leiden)
Orientalistische Litteraturzeitung (Berlin)
Oriente Moderno (Roma)
Ostasiatische Rundschau (Shanghai)
Osteuropa (Stuttgart)

Pakistan Library Association Quarterly Journal (Lahore)
Petermanns Geographische Mitteilungen (Gotha)
Philological Society, see Trans. Philol. Soc.
Philosophical Transactions of the Royal Society (London)
Poradnik Jezykowy (Warszawa)
Prilozi za Orijentalnu Filologiju i Istoriju (Sarajevo)
Problemy Vostokovedenija (Moskva)
Proceedings of the British Academy (London)
Przegład Biblioteczny (Kraków)
Przegład Orientalistyczny (Warszawa)

Regional Cultural Institute (Iran, Pakistan, Turkey), see
    J. Reg. Cult. Inst. Iran
Renseignements Coloniaux; supplément au Bulletin Mensuel du Comite de
    l'Afrique Française (Paris)
Review of Reviews (New York)
Revista Arhivelor (Bucureşti)
Revista de Estudios Clásicos (Mendoza)
Revue de la Documentation ('s Gravenhage)
Revue de l'Ecole Nationale des Langues Orientales (Paris)
Revue de Phonétique Appliquée (Mons, Belgique)
Revue des Etudes Islamiques (Paris)
Revue du Monde Musulman (Paris)
Revue Hispanique (Paris)
Revue Internationale des Etudes Balkaniques (Beograd)
Revue Roumaine de Géologie, Géophysique et Géographie. Série de
    Géographie (Bucureşti)
Revue Tunisienne (Tunis)
Rivista Italo-Bulgara di Letteratura, Storia, Arte (Sofia)
Rocznik Orientalistyczny (Lwów)
Romania (Paris)
Royal Asiatic Society, see J. Roy. Asiat. Soc.
Royal Society, see Phil. Trans. Roy. Soc.
Russischunterricht (Berlin)

School of Oriental and African Studies, see
    Bull. Sch. Orient. Afr. Stud.
Science (Cambridge, Mass.)
Sefarad (Madrid)

Seminar für Orientalische Sprachen, see
    Mitt. Seminar Orient. Sprach.
Sitzungsberichte der philosophisch-historischen Classe der Kaiserlichen
    Akademie der Wissenschaften (Wien)
Slavia (Praha)
Slavia Orientalis (Warszawa)
Slavonic and East European Review (London)
The Slavonic Review (London)
Slovenska Reč (Bratislava)
Sociedade de Geographia de Lisboa. Boletim (Lisboa)
Societé de Linguistique de Paris, see
    Bull. Soc. Linguist. Paris
    Mem. Soc. Linguist. Paris
South African Library Quarterly Bulletin (Cape Town)
Sovetskaja Bibliografija (Moskva)
Special Libraries (New York)
Sprawozdania z Posiedzeń Towarzystwa Naukowego Warszawskiego.
    Wydział 1: Językoznawstwa i Historii Literatury (Warszawa)
Studia et Acta Orientalia (București)
Studia Slavica Academiae Scientiarum Hungaricae (Budapest)
Studies in Linguistics (New Haven, Conn.)
Studii Teologice (București)
Südostforschungen (München)
Swarajya (Madras)
Systematic Zoology (New Haven, Conn.)

Taškentskij Gosudarstvennyj Universitet, see
    Nauč. Trudy Taškent. Gos. Univ., Filol. Nauk
Taxon (Utrecht)
Tetradi Perevodčika (Moskva)
Teuthonista (Halle/Saale)
Toshokan Kenkyu (Osaka)
T'oung Pao (Leiden)
Transactions and Proceedings of the Japan Society (London)
Transactions of the Philological Society (London)
Trudy Akademija Nauk S.S.S.R. Sibirskoe Otdelenie (Moskva)

Učenje Zapiski. Serija Filologičeskih Nauk. Leningradskogo Universiteta
    (Leningrad)
Unesco Bulletin for Libraries (Paris)
Universität Rostock, see Wiss. Z. Univ. Rostock, Ges. Sprachwiss.
University of Wisconsin Library News (Madison, Wis.)
Ural-altaische Jahrbücher (Wiesbaden)

Vermessungstechnik (Berlin)
Verwaltung (Stuttgart)
Vestnik Leningradskogo Universiteta. Serija Biologii, Geografii i
    Geologii (Leningrad)
Visible Language (Cleveland, Ohio)
Voprosy Jazykoznanija (Moskva)
Voprosy Kul'turi Reči (Moskva)
Vostočnij Sbornik (Leningrad)

Washington Academy of Sciences, see J. Wash. Acad. Sci.
Die Welt des Orients (Göttingen)
Die wissenschaftliche Redaktion (Mannheim)
Wissenschaftliche Zeitschrift der Humboldt-Universität zu Berlin.
   Gesellschafts- und Sprachwissenschaftliche Reihe. (Berlin)
Wissenschaftliche Zeitschrift der Universität Rostock. Gesellschafts-
   und Sprachwissenschaften. (Rostock)

Yad Lakore (Jerusalem)

Z.I.I.D. Zeitschrift (Berlin)
Zeitschrift der Deutschen Morgenländischen Gesellschaft (Leipzig)
Zeitschrift für Bibliothekswesen und Bibliographie (Frankfurt/Main)
Zeitschrift für Mundartforschung (Halle/Saale)
Zeitschrift für Phonetik und allgemeine Sprachwissenschaft (Berlin)
Zentralblatt für Bibliothekswesen (Leipzig)
Zentralinstitut für Information und Dokumentation, see Z.I.I.D.
Zikhronot ha-Aqademya (Jerusalem)

ii) Festschriften

Slavisch-deutsche Wechselbeziehungen in Sprache, Literatur und Kultur.
   Festschrift Hans Holm BIELFELDT. Berlin: Akademie-Verlag, 1969.

Mélanges Hartwig DERENBOURG. Paris, 1909.

Professor P.K. GODE commemorative volume. Poona, 1960. (Poona Oriental
   series no. 93)

To honor Roman JAKOBSON. Essays on the occasion of his 70th birthday.
   The Hague: Mouton 1967. (Janua linguarum, series minor 32)

Studies presented to LI CHI in honour of his 70th birthday. Taipeh:
   Tsing-Hua Journal Publication Committee, 1965-67.

Homenaje a MILLÁS-VALLICROSA. Barcelona, 1954, 1956.

Collectanea Mongolica. Festschrift für Prof. Dr. RINTCHEN ...
   Asiatische Forschungen, 17, 1966.

I.J.S. TARAPOREWALA memorial volume. Madras: Linguistic Society of
   India, 1957.

iii) Conference Proceedings and Other Collective Works

Association of Jewish Libraries. Annual convention. 4th, Atlantic City, 1969.

Conference on American Library Resources on Southern Asia. Washington, D.C., 1957.

The Field of Yiddish. New York, McGraw-Hill, 1954. (Publication of the Linguistic Circle of New York, 3)

International Conference on Cataloguing Principles. Paris, 1961. London: IFLA, 1963.

International Conference Seminar of Tamil Studies. Kuala Lumpur: University of Malaya, 1968-69.

International Congress of Orientalists.

International Federation for Documentation. International conference.

International Geographical Congress.

Language standardization. The Hague: Mouton, 1963. (Janua linguarum, series minor 29)

Lautzeichen und ihre Anwendung in verschiedenen Sprachgebieten. Berlin: Reichsdruckerei, 1928.

Orfografija sobstvennyh imen. Moskva: "Nauka", 1964.

Probleme der neugriechischen Literatur. Berlin: Akademie-Verlag, 1959. (Berliner byzantinische Arbeiten 14-17)

Die Reform der Nationalschriften. Wolfenbüttel: Heckner, 1932. (Archiv für Schreib- und Buchwesen, Sondernummer 5)

Russkij jazyk, literatura, metodika. Praha: Státní pedagog. naklad., 1965.

Slavjanskaja leksikografija i leksikologija. Moskva: "Nauka", 1966.

Studien zur Geschichte der russischen Literatur des 18. Jahrhunderts. Berlin: Akademie-Verlag, 1968. (Veröffentlichungen des Instituts für Slawistik der Deutschen Akademie zu Berlin, 28)

Toponomastika i transkripcija. Moskva: "Nauka", 1964.

Transkripcija geografičeskih nazvanij. Moskva: "Nauka", 1960.

Voprosy filologij istoričeskij strany sovetskij zarubežnaja vostoka. Moskva: "Nauka", 1961

Voprosy terminologii. Moskva: Akademija Nauk S.S.S.R., 1961.

BIBLIOGRAPHY ON TRANSCRIPTION AND TRANSLITERATION

BIBLIOGRAPHY ON TRANSCRIPTION AND TRANSLITERATION

I. GENERALITIES

Scripts

1
De literis sive characteribus, ipsarum usu mirabilis, origine et inventione prima et diversitate in linguis praecipuis. [On letters or characters, their marvellous use, origin and first invention, and their diversity in the principal languages.] In Biblia polyglotta ... London, 1657, v. 1, Prolegomena ii, p. 6-14.
   This polyglot Bible was edited by Bishop Bryan Walton. The chapter on various scripts contains comparative tables of transliteration. It has been attributed to John Owen.

2
WILKINS, J. An essay towards a real character, and a philosophical language. London, 1668. 454 p.
   An attempt to create a universal language, written in a universal script.

3
LODWICK, F. An essay towards an universal alphabet (together with a further essay concerning an universal primer, to which is added a specimen of a new character fitted to the said alphabet...) Philosophical Transactions, 16, no. 182, 1688:126-137.

4
EICHHOFF, F.G. Parallèle des langues d'Europe et de l'Inde ... avec un essai de transcription générale. [Comparison between the languages of Europe and India... with an attempt at a general transcription.] Paris, Imprimerie royale, 1836. vii, 499 p.
   See also 6.

5
MATUŠÍK, A. Alphabetum et orthographia universalis, ex naturae et artis observationibus deducta ... [Universal alphabet and orthography, deducted from observations of nature and art.] Rozniaviae, 1837.

6
EICHHOFF, F.G. Vergleichung der Sprachen von Europa und Indien ... nebst einem Versuch einer allgemeinen Umschreibung der Sprachen ... [Comparison between the languages of Europe and India ... with an attempt at a general transcription of languages.] Leipzig, Weber, 1840. xiv, 354 p.

7
ELLIS, A.J. The essentials of phonetics, containing the theory of a universal alphabet, together with its practical

application to the reduction of all languages ... to one
uniform system of writing ... London, Pitman, 1848.
   One of the earliest attempts at the creation of a phonetic alphabet. The work appeared in several editions, in
   each of which the author introduced changes and "improvements".

8
VENN, H. Rules for reducing unwritten languages to alphabetical writing in Roman characters, with reference especially to the languages spoken in Africa. London, Church
Missionary Society, 1848.

9
LEPSIUS, K.R. Uebertragung fremder Schriftsysteme und bis-
her noch ungeschriebener Sprachen in europäische Buchstaben.
Berlin, W. Hertz, 1855. 64 p.
   A much enlarged English translation was published in 1863,
      see 14. The first scientifically sound phonetic alphabet.

10
MÜLLER, F.M. The languages of the seat of war in the East.
With a survey of the three families of language: Semitic,
Asian, and Turanian... 2nd ed., with an appendix on the miss-
ionary alphabet ... London, Williams & Norgate, 1855. xcvi,
150 p.

11
ELLIS, A.J. Universal writing and printing with ordinary
letters for the use of missionaries, comparative philologists,
linguists and phonologists ... London, Pitman, 1856.
   A comparative table of scripts on p. 22.

12
SCHÜTZ, F. De l'alphabet universel; examen des essais de
Ch. de Brosses, de Volney et de M. Lepsius. [On the univer-
sal alphabet; review of the attempts by Ch. de Brosses, de
Volney and Mr. Lepsius.] Nancy, Grimblot, 1859. 84 p.

13
THOMPSON, J.G. Pointed and unpointed Romanic alphabets com-
pared in six versions of Luke xiv, 18-20. Mangalore, German
Mission Press, 1859. 6 p.
   Transliterations of these N.T. verses from Malayalam, Ta-
      mil, Telugu, Kannada and Hindi.

14
LEPSIUS, K.R. Standard alphabet for reducing unwritten languages and foreign graphic systems to a uniform orthography in
European letters. London, Williams & Norgate, 1863. xvii,
315 p.

15
SCHLEIERMACHER, A.A.E. Das harmonische oder allgemeine Alphabet zur Transcription fremder Schriftsysteme in lateinische Schrift, zunächst in seiner Anwendung auf die slawischen
und semitischen Sprachen. [The harmonic or general alphabet

for the transcription of foreign scripts into Roman script,
at first in its application to the Slavic and Semitic languages.] Darmstadt, Jonghaus, 1864. xxiv, 568 p.

16
BACHMAIER, A. Pasigraphisches Wörterbuch zum Gebrauche für die deutsche Sprache. Augsburg, 1868. 2 v.
   A proposal for an ideographic universal script, largely based on numerals. The author himself translated the work into English and French:

17
BACHMAIER, A. Dictionnaire pasigraphique précédé de la grammaire ... Augsburg, 1868. 2 v.

18
BACHMAIER, A. Pasigraphical dictionary and grammar. Augsburg, Volkhart, 1870. 2 v.

19
Universal syllabics; a new method for learning to read, applicable to all languages. In The Lord's Prayer in three hundred languages ... with a preface by Reinhold Rost. London, Gilbert & Rivington, 1891. p. 85.

20
S., E.J. De l'alphabet universel, au sujet de la réforme projetée de l'orthographe ... [About the universal alphabet, on the subject of the planned reform of orthography.] Paris, 1893. 24 p.

21
MORRIS, H. Alphabet for languages not yet reduced to writing. J. Roy. Asiat. Soc., 1898:23-28.

22
SCHRAMM, A., ed. Die Reform der Nationalschriften. Beiträge zur Reform der türkischen, russischen, chinesischen und japanischen Schrift. [The reform of national scripts; contributions on the reform of the Turkish, Russian, Chinese and Japanese scripts.] Wolfenbüttel, Heckner, 1932. 44 p. (Sondernummer 5, Archiv für Schreib- und Buchwesen)
   See also 291, 506, 586, 587.

23
PAVEK, W.J. 200,000,000 Slavs need a new alphabet. Detroit, S.J. Bloch, 1944. 105 p.

24
PARSELL, J.R. World fonetic alfabet. 3rd ed. New York, 1946. 94 p.

25
PARSELL, J.R. An alfabet for the world of tomorrow. 3rd ed. Kansas City, 1947. 64 p.

26
NOUGAYROL, J. Notices sur les caractères étrangers. [Notes on foreign characters.] 2e éd. Paris, Imprimerie nationale, 1948. xv, 427 p.

27
PARSELL, J.R. One alfabet. Kansas City, 1948. 170 p.
  This edition contains 24 and 25 as Part 1 and 2; part 3 is entitled "World alfabet sistem". One of the more whimsical attempts at creating a universal alphabet, suitable for "all" languages. It is almost entirely based on English.

28
HENZE, P.B. Alphabet changes in Soviet Central Asia and Communist China. J. Roy. Cent. Asian Soc., April 1957:124-136.

29
WALTER, A.J. Schriftentwicklung unter dem Einfluss der Diktaturen. [Development of scripts under the influence of dictatorships.] Mitt. Inst. österr. Geschichtsforsch., 68, 1960:337-361.
  Contents: 1. Schrift als Konvention. 2. Kemal Atatürk. 3. Stalin. 4. Der chinesische Reformplan. 5. Hitler. 6. Von der Fraktur zur Universalschrift des 20. Jahrhunderts.

30
MUSAEV, K.M. [Alphabets of the languages of the peoples of the U.S.S.R.] Moskva, "Nauka", 1965. 85 p. (In Russian)
  Comparative treatment of the various alphabets now used in the Soviet Union, most of which are based on the Cyrillic alphabet. Contains an English summary.

31
RATHER, L.J. Special characters and diacritical marks used in Roman alphabets. Library Resources and Technical Services, 12, Summer 1968:285-295.
  The most comprehensive summary to date on all diacritical marks used. The study was undertaken in connection with the development of a special print chain for the production of entries from MARC tapes in the Library of Congress.

32
SCHRÖPFER, J. Hussens Traktat "Orthographia Bohemica"; die Herkunft des diakritischen Systems in der Schreibung slavischer Sprachen und die älteste zusammenhängende Beschreibung slavischer Laute. [The tractate "Orthographia Bohemica" by Hus; the origin of the diacritical system for the writing of Slavic languages and the oldest comprehensive description of Slavic sounds.] Wiesbaden, Harrassowitz, 1968. 142 p.
  A critical edition of Jan Hus' treatise, in which he states that the Latin alphabet is insufficient to express the sounds of the Bohemian language and introduces the diacritical signs still used today in the Czech language.

33
LOTZ, J. Comment: the role of script in describing the languages of the world. Visible Language, 5, no. 1, Winter 1971: 75-81.
***
See also 53, 63, 64, 109, 110, 111, 112, 114, 172, 463.

Transliteration and transcription (general)

34
MÜLLER, F. Die Transcription fremder Alphabete. [The transcription of foreign alphabets.] Sitzungsber. Phil.-Hist. Cl. Kaiserl. Akad. Wiss., 136, 1897. 12 p.
   A criticism of the transliteration scheme proposed by Kuhn and Schnorr von Carolsfeld (see 66), and counter-proposal using Greek letters and many diacritical marks. Eight tables for as many groups of languages (but Slavic languages are not included).

35
GLEICHEN, E. Foreign languages transcribed into English, according to the RGS II system, by E. Gleichen and J.H. Reynolds. London, Royal Geographical Society, 1921. xv, 71 p. (R.G.S. Technical series no. 2)
   This transliteration system and later elaborations of it is now the most widely used one for geographical purposes. See also 44.

36
Phonetic transcription and transliteration. Proposals of the Copenhagen conference, April 1925. Oxford, Clarendon Press, 1926. 32 p.

37
Phonetische Transkription und Transliteration. Nach den Verhandlungen der Kopenhagener Konferenz im April 1925. Uebersetzung von K. Meinhof. Heidelberg, Winter, 1926. 36 p.

38
Transcription phonétique et translittération. Propositions établies par la conférence tenue á Copenhague en avril 1925. Oxford, Clarendon Press, 1926.
   The proposals of this conference, published simultaneously in three languages, formed the basis for the present international phonetic alphabet (IPA).

39
FORCHHAMMER, J. Ergebnis der Kopenhagener Konferenz zur Lösung der phonetischen Transkriptionsfrage im Lichte der neuen Phonetik. [Results of the Copenhagen conference on the solution of phonetic transcription in the light of modern phonetics.] Germanisch-romanische Monatsschrift, 15, 1927:385-395.

40
WHARTON, L.C. Transcriptions of foreign tongues. Trans. Philol. Soc., 1921-1924:59-112.
   Considers five different purposes of transliteration and examines critically the various schemes proposed until the early '20ies. Extensive bibliography on p. 59-112.

41
WHARTON, L.C. Remarks on the Copenhagen scheme of phonetic transcription and transliteration of 1925. Trans. Philol. Soc., 1925-1930:292-299.

42
COMMISSION INTERNATIONALE DE COOPÉRATION INTELLECTUELLE.
L'adoption universelle des caractères latins. [The universal adoption of Roman characters.] Paris, 1934. (Dossiers de la coopération intellectuelle)

43
WHARTON, L.C. Transliteration or transcription. Trans. Int. Fed. Docum., 14, 1938:244-245.
   Surveys ancient and modern transliteration schemes and their problems. Recommends transliteration (if necessary supplemented by diacritical marks) to enable unambiguous re-transliteration.

44
GLEICHEN, E. Alphabets of foreign languages transcribed into English, according to the RGS II system, by E. Gleichen and J.H. Reynolds. 2nd ed., reprinted with incorporation of supplement of 1938 and certain revisions by M. Aurousseau... London, Royal Geographical Society, 1944. xvi, 82 p. (Royal Geographical Society Technical series no. 2)
   This was reprinted by the Permanent Committee on Geographical Names in 1956.

45
ŠEVČIK, A. Translittération. Revue de la Documentation, 14, 1947:21-22.

46
VON OSTERMANN, G.F. Manual of foreign languages for the use of librarians, bibliographers, research workers, editors, translators and printers. 4th ed. rev. New York, Central Book Co., 1952. 414 p.
   The most comprehensive listing of alphabets. All non-Roman scripts are transliterated. Has a table of diacritical marks showing the languages which use them in addition to Roman characters. Unfortunately, this reference work is now out of print.

47
AVANESOV, R.I. [On three types of scientific linguistic transcription.] Slavia, 25, 1956:347-371. (In Russian)
   Distinguishes three types of transcription: phonetic, lexico-phonemic and morpho-phonemic. Review, see 50.

49
KENT, F.L. International progress in transliteration. Unesco Bulletin for Libraries, 10, May-June 1956:132-137.
   Summarizes ISO's work in the field and discusses some of the problems involved on the international level.

50
GVOZDEV, A.N. [The phonetic question: on three types of transcription.] Voprosy Jazykoznanija, 6, 1958:76-86. (In Russian)
   A review and critique of 47.

51
SUPERANSKAJA, A.V. [The international alphabet and international transcription.] <u>Voprosy Jazykoznanija</u>, <u>7</u>, 1958:78-85. (In Russian)

52
MEYRIAT, J. La normalisation internationale des codes de translittération. [The international standardization of transliteration codes.] <u>Courrier de la Normalisation</u>, <u>27</u>, 1960:593-596.

53
VASIL'KOV, B.P. On the Latinization of authors' names written after the names of taxa. <u>Taxon</u>, <u>7</u>, 1960:199-200.
 Proposes amendments to the "International Code of Botanical Nomenclature" regarding the transliteration of names written in non-Roman alphabets or whose names contain letters without equivalent in the Latin alphabet.

54
FRONTARD, R. Transliteration codes and their international standardization. <u>Unesco Bulletin for Libraries</u>, <u>15</u>, March-April 1961:78-82.
 On progress in ISO's work. Discusses the principles of transliteration, its terminology, and the difficulties encountered in non-vocalized scripts (Arabic and Hebrew).

55
MINISSI, N. Principi di trascrizione. [Principles of transcription.] Napoli, Pironti, 1961. 44 p.

56
DOROSZEWSKI, W. O transliteracji; objaśnienia wyraźow i zwrotow. [On transliteration; explanation of words and phrases.] <u>Poradnik Językowy</u>, no. 5/6, 1962:285-287.

57
LAZAREK, W. Normalizacja transliteracji i transkrypcji. [Standardization of transliteration and transcription.] <u>Normalizacja,</u> 1963:243-244.

58
INTERNATIONAL ORGANIZATION FOR STANDARDIZATION. General principles for the conversion of one written language into another. (ISO/TC 46 (Sec. 426) 697 (Rev.))
 A revised version of an earlier "Introductory note on the general principles of transliteration", first published in ISO/R9 (see 222), and approved in 1964. It is now reprinted in all ISO recommendations on transliteration.

59
CATFORD, J.C. A linguistic theory of translation; an essay in applied linguistics. London, Oxford University Press, 1965. 103 p.
 Chapter 10. Transliteration, gives a brief linguistic exposition of the subject and defines transliteration and transcription.

60
MANGOLD, M. Transliteration und Transkription. [Transliteration and transcription.] Mannheim, Bibliographisches Institut, 1965. 17 p.
   Discusses "popular" versus "scientific" Romanization of various scripts, with emphasis on the Cyrillic alphabet as transliterated for German readers. Also published as

61
MANGOLD, M. Transliteration und Transkription. Die wissenschaftliche Redaktion, 1, 1965:77-89.

62
UNITED STATES. GOVERNMENT PRINTING OFFICE. Style manual. Rev. ed. Washington, 1967. 512 p.
   Ch. 25. Foreign languages, deals with the transcription of Greek (classical and modern), Hebrew and Russian, following the U.S. Board of Geographic Names scheme, with exceptions due to Library of Congress practice noted. There is also a separate section on "Slavic languages and their alphabets".

63
DIRINGER, D. The alphabet; a key to the history of mankind. 3rd ed. New York, Funk & Wagnall, 1968. 2 v.
   The most comprehensive work on the origin and history of scripts. Transliteration is dealt with briefly in the introduction. The adaptation of the Cyrillic alphabet to non-Slavic languages is discussed at some length on p. 378-381. Vol. 2 is entirely devoted to specimens of almost all scripts treated in vol. 1.

64
GERMANY. BUNDESDRUCKEREI. Alphabete und Schriftzeichen des Morgen- und des Abendlandes; zum allgemeinen Gebrauch, mit besonderer Berücksichtigung des Buchgewerbes. [Alphabets and scripts of Orient and Occident; for general use, with special regard to typography.] 2. Aufl. Berlin, 1969. 107 p.
   Lists alphabets of 86 languages, of which 57 are in non-Roman scripts with transliteration tables.

Bibliographical and library work

65
AMERICAN LIBRARY ASSOCIATION. COMMITTEE ON TRANSLITERATION. Report. In Lake George Conference proceedings. Library J., 10, 1885:302-311.
   The report was read by Cutter and was followed by a discussion which showed that the whole problem was considered to be a somewhat amusing oddity. There are several tables of transliteration for Sanskrit, Russian and Semitic languages, all of which are reproduced from not very legible handwriting (the printer apparently had no suitable type). See also 85, 86.

66
KUHN, E.W.A. and SCHNORR VON CAROLSFELD, H. Die Transscription fremder Alphabete. Vorschläge zur Lösung der Frage auf Grund des Genfer "Rapport de la Commission de transcription" und mit Berücksichtigung von Bibliothekszwecken. [The transcription of foreign alphabets; proposals for the solution of the problem, based on the Geneva "Rapport de la Commission de transcription" and with regard to library purposes.] Leipzig, 1897. 15 p.
   The first comprehensive attempt at a solution suitable for library purposes. There are tables for Sanskrit, Armenian, Arabic, Persian, Turkish, Hindustani, Afghanic, Malay, Hebrew, Syriac, Ethiopian, Coptic, and the Slavic languages. For the Geneva report, see 98, 99.

67
SOMMER, F.E. Transliteration problems. Library J., 58, June 15, 1933:534-536.
   States that the transliteration schemes used are a "permanent source of confusion". Gives examples from Russian, Arabic, and Chinese, and deals also with re-transliteration. Makes a plea for strict and "scientific" standardization.

68
SOMMER, F.E. Books in foreign script in the public library. Library J., 59, Nov. 15, 1934:892-893.

69
La transliteración de alfabetos no latinos. [The transliteration of non-Roman alphabets.] Boletin de Bibliotecas y de Bibliografía, 2, 1935:236-243.

70
SOMMER, F.E. Co-ordinated transliteration in libraries. Library Quart., 7, October 1937:492-501.
   The principles used in transliteration are far from uniform. Most inconsistencies stem from an endeavour to bring out the pronunciation, and from the use of symbols by different languages. Aims should be: use of one Roman letter for each foreign character (reversibility); use of diacritical marks; and international cooperation.

71
RANGANATHAN, S.R. Theory of library catalogue. Madras, Madras Library Association, 1938. 393 p.
   Transliteration is treated on p. 284-287. This is the first textbook on library practice to deal with the problem in depth.

72
SHAW, E.P. Transliteration: a game for the library sleuth. Bull. Med. Libr. Ass., 37, April 1949:142-145.

73
MAIMON, Z. [A general catalog or a catalog by language.] Yad Lakore, 4, 1956/1957:128-129. (In Hebrew)
   Discusses the pros and cons of a unified Hebrew catalog versus a catalog divided by kinds of script.

74
KALAN, P. Choice of entry for authors whose names vary. In International conference on cataloguing principles. Paris, 1961. London, IFLA, 1963. p. 219-227.
   Discusses the problem of authors who write in different scripts.

75
MEUVRET, C. Translittération, transcription: le point de vue de la bibliothèque. [Transliteration, transcription: the viewpoint of the library.] Revue de l'Ecole Nationale des Langues Orientales, 1, 1964:111-117.

76
PIETTE, J.R.F. A guide to foreign languages for science librarians and bibliographers. London, Aslib, 1965. 53 p.
   This deals only incidentally with transliteration. Both the B.S. and the ISO scheme are given for Slavic languages.

77
CENTER FOR APPLIED LINGUISTICS. The Linguistic Bibliography project; informal progress report for the period Aug.2, 1965-May 1, 1966. Washington, D.C., 1966.
   Appendix B. Transliterations used in the L.B., p. 36-48, deals with Arabic, Chinese, Japanese, Korean and Cyrillic and has tables for each of these scripts. Appendix D. Transliterations, transcriptions and related problems, with special reference to the L.B., by Kathleen Lewis (1964), p. 58-61.

78
WRIGHT, H.C. Metagraphy and graphic priority; a discursus for catalogers. Cleveland, Case Western Reserve University, 1969. 348 p. (Ph.D. thesis) University Microfilm order no. 70-26,012.
   Poses two questions: (1) Why transliterate? (2) How can bibliographical confusion be eliminated in transcription? The first question is analyzed in terms of cultural pluralism and the need for consistency in the identification and indexing of bibliographical items; the second one is answered in terms of the separate realms of spoken and written language and the graphic nature of bibliography.

79
RABENSTEIN, B.H. A survey on the use of alphabetical forms in author and/or title headings in the catalogs of Israeli libraries. Washington, D.C., Catholic University, 1970. 102 l. (MLS thesis)
   On transliteration problems encountered in Hebrew-language catalogs. Apparently written without any first-hand knowledge of actual Hebrew catalogs. Proposes the adoption of Romanization as the best ultimate solution. A critical review by R. Tronik appeared in Yad Lakore, 12, no. 2, 1972:122-124.

80
BLANKEN, R.R. The preparation of international author indexes, with particular reference to the problems of transliteration, prefixes, and compound family names. <u>J. Amer. Soc. Inform. Sci.</u>, <u>22</u>, Jan.-Feb. 1971:51-63.

81
MEHTA, J.C. Problems of the multi-language, multi-script library: cataloguing in Delhi Public Library. <u>International Cataloguing</u>, <u>2</u>, Jan.-March 1973:5-6.
   The problems of cataloging Oriental names written in various scripts and in many different forms.

82
SIEW, KEE YEH and CHANG SOH CHOO. Problems of the multi-language, multi-script library: multi-language catalogues in the National Library, Singapore. Liverpool, IFLA Council 1971. 25 p.
   The transliteration problem in a library serving a polyglot community. The catalogs for different scripts are kept separately, with some cross-referencing. The compilation of the <u>Singapore National Bibliography</u> and the filing of entries are discussed, and examples of entries are shown. There is an extensive bibliography on the cataloging of works in Chinese, Malayalam, and Tamil. A condensed version of this paper appeared in <u>International Cataloguing</u>, <u>1</u>, no.2, 1972:7-8; no. 3:5-7.

83
STIPČEVIĆ, A. The new Yugoslav Cataloguing Rules and their application in Yugoslav libraries. Liverpool, IFLA Council, 1971. 3 p.
   The transliteration problems of one language written in two scripts. Where books in both scripts are held by libraries, two separate catalogs are kept. Problems in re-transliteration of foreign names for the national bibliography. A condensed version of this paper appeared in <u>International Cataloguing</u>, <u>1</u>, no. 3, 1972:7-8.

***

See also 119, 122, 221, 308, 311, 344, 355, 417, 450, 459, 490, 514, 519, 529, 534, 542, 545, 556, 557, 561, 629, 630, 631, 637.

Catalog codes and rules

84
HOFBIBLIOTHEK. Wien. Vorschrift für die Verfassung des alphabetischen Nominalzettelkatalogs der Druckwerke der K.K. Hofbibliothek ... [Rules for the compilation of the alphabetical card catalog of names for printed works in the Imperial and Royal Court Library.] Wien, 1901. 1 v.
   Beilage I. Vorschrift für die Transscription fremder Schriftarten [Appendix I. Rules for the transcription of foreign scripts], p. 62-68. Contains tables for

Ethiopian, Arabic, Afghan, Hindustani, Malayalam, Persian, Turkish, Armenian, Georgian, Hebrew, Zend, Huzvareš (Pehlevi), Coptic, Sanskrit, Glagolitic, Bulgarian, Russian, Serbian, Syrian (Estrangelo). Greek has no transliteration table, but Rule 41 states that it is to be rendered "in Erasmic transcription".

85
CUTTER, C.A. Rules for a dictionary catalog. 4th ed. Washington, D.C., Govt. Print. Off., 1904.
Rule 37. Transliteration, p. 37-39. A reprint of the Report and transliteration tables for Sanskrit, Cyrillic characters and other languages, taken from 65 above, is appended; for Hebrew and Arabic, the system used by the Jewish Encyclopedia of 1902, v. 2, p. ix-x is recommended (but no tables are given).

86
AMERICAN LIBRARY ASSOCIATION. Catalog rules; author and title entries. American ed. Chicago, 1908. 88 p.
The Report (see 65) is again reprinted, followed by tables for Ethiopian, Arabic, Syriac, Hebrew, Slavic, Sanskrit and Modern Greek on p. 69-73.

87
Instruktionen für die alphabetischen Kataloge der Preussischen Bibliotheken vom 10. Mai 1899. 2. Ausgabe in der Fassung vom 10. August 1908. Wiesbaden, Harrassowitz, 1966. x, 179 p. (Unveränderter Nachdruck)
Has tables of transliteration for Russian, Ukrainian, Old Bulgarian, New Bulgarian, Serbian, Romanian, Sanskrit, Arabic, Persian, Turkish, Hindustani, Malayalam, Hebrew, Syriac, Ethiopian, Coptic, Armenian and Georgian on p. 142-148. Greek has no table, but Rule 22.2 gives some instructions for particular letters and diphthongs.
A complete English translation of the code appeared as

87a
The Prussian instructions: rules for the alphabetical catalogues of the Prussian libraries; translated from the 2nd ed. by Andrew Osborn. Ann Arbor, Univ. of Michigan Press, 1938.

88
BRITISH MUSEUM. DEPARTMENT OF PRINTED BOOKS. Rules for compiling the catalogue of printed books, maps and music in the British Museum. London, 1936.
Transliteration of Gaelic names. Transliteration of Slavonic, Roumanian and modern Greek names, p. 50-56.

89
BIBLIOTECA APOSTOLICA VATICANA. Norme per il catalogo degli stampati. Roma, 1939.
Transliteration tables for Arabic, Persian, Turkish, Armenian, Coptic, Ethiopic, Gaelic, Greek, Hebrew, Slavic languages and Syriac. A complete English translation appeared in 1948 under the title

Vatican Library. Rules for the catalog of printed books. Chicago, American Library Association, 1948.

90
AMERICAN LIBRARY ASSOCIATION. A.L.A. Cataloging rules for author and title entries ... 2nd ed., edited by Clara Beetle. Chicago, 1949. 265 p.
   Tables of transliteration for Slavic languages (Russian, Ukrainian, White-Russian, Bulgarian, Serbian), Modern Greek, Semitic (Arabic and Hebrew), with additional notes on Hebrew and Yiddish. The tables are preceded by an explanation of the "Rules of the new Russian orthography" and the necessary changes in transliteration from Russian. The subsequent "Cataloging rules of the A.L.A. and the Library of Congress, additions and changes 1949-1958" (Washington, D.C., 1959) contain several additional transliteration tables, particularly for Chinese, Jananese and Korean (see 618); most of these were later superseded by transliteration tables published by the Library of Congress in its Cataloging Service. For these, see under individual languages and scripts.

91
TURKEY. MAARIF VEKÂLETI. Yazma ve eski basma kitapların tasnif ve fişleme kılavuzu ve İslâm dini ilimleri tasnif cetveli. [Guide to the classification and cataloging of manuscripts and old books, and classification tables for Islamica.] Istabul, Maarif Basımevi, 1958. 50 p.
   Contains rules for the transliteration of Turkish written in Arabic characters into Latinized Turkish.

92
WAGNER, E. Regeln für die alphabetische Katalogisierung von Druckschriften in den islamischen Sprachen (arabisch, persisch, türkisch) ... [Rules for the alphabetical cataloging of printed works in the Islamic languages (Arabic, Persian, Turkish.] Wiesbaden, Harassowitz, 1961. 73 p.
   This supplements and updates the rules in 87. H. Braun (490) considers these rules to be very practical and useful, but E. Birnbaum (514) finds them "sketchy", subject to various interpretations and not suitable for Ottoman Turkish.

93
RANGANATHAN, S.R. Classified catalogue code, with additional rules for dictionary catalogue code. 5th ed. Bombay, Asia Publishing House, 1964. 644 p.
   On various scripts and the transliteration problem, p. 67-68, 93.

94
SPAIN. DIRECCION GENERAL DE ARCHIVOS Y BIBLIOTECAS. Instrucciones para la redaccion del catalogo alfabetico de autores y obras anonimas en las bibliotecas publicas del estado. [Instructions for the compilation of the alpha-

betical catalog of authors and anonymous works in the public libraries of the state.] 3a ed. reformada. Madrid, 1964.
> Rule 8. Libros en caracteres no latinos [Books in non-Roman characters] deals with transliteration.

Re-transliteration

95
PODBORNY, J.G. Die Rückübertragung nichtrussischer Namen aus der russischen in die lateinische Schrift. [The re-transliteration of non-Russian names from the Russian into the Roman script.] Babel, 7, no. 1, 1961:13-23.

96
LÖHR, H. Transliteration japanischer Wörter über die kyrillische in die lateinische Schrift. [Transliteration of Japanese words into Roman script via the Cyrillic.] Informatik, 18, Nr. 5, 1971:48-52.
> Because of the syllabic structure of Japanese, the form of words transliterated from Japanese directly into Roman differs from the same words transliterated into Roman script via the Cyrillic; this occurs when citations in the Russian Referativnyj Žurnal are re-processed for Western information systems which contain Japanese citations transliterated directly, and has very serious consequences for retrieval. A concordance list of Japanese syllables in direct Romanization and in Cyrillization is given as an aid for conversion.

***

See also 80, 344, 355.

II. INDO-EUROPEAN LANGUAGES
INDO-ARYAN LANGUAGES
Sanskrit

97
WILLIAMS, M. Applications of the Roman alphabet to the expression of Sanskrit and other Eastern languages. An address ... delivered to the [5th] International Congress of Orientalists, Berlin, Sept. 14, 1881. London, Allen, 1881. 9-14 p.

98
ROYAL ASIATIC SOCIETY. TRANSLITERATION COMMITTEE. Report of the Transliteration Committee. J. Roy. Asiat. Soc., 1894. 13 p.
> Transliteration of Sanskrit, Pali and Arabic, with some additions for other languages.

99
INTERNATIONAL CONGRESS OF ORIENTALISTS. 10th, Geneva, 1894. Report of the Transliteration Committee (Translation).

J. Roy. Asiat. Soc., 1895:879-889.
   Transliteration of Sanskrit and Prakrit, proposals for a
   transliteration scheme for Arabic, and a note by G.T.
   Plunkett on the work of the Committee whose members represented British, French and German orientalists.

100
LIBRARY OF CONGRESS. Sanskrit and Prakrit in Devanagari
script. Cataloging Service, Bulletin 64, Feb. 1964, p. 17.

101
CHATTERJI, S.K. Sanskrit in Perso-Arabic script: a side-
light on the medieval pronunciation of Sanskrit in Kashmir
and Northern India. Indian Linguistics, 7, 1939:133-166.

102
HAMILTON, C.H. K'uei Chi's commentary on Wei-Shi-es-Shi-Lun.
J. Amer. Oriental Soc., 53, no. 2, June 1933:144-151.
   On the transliteration of a Sanskrit text into Chinese.

103
PULLEYBLANCK, E.G. The transcription of Sanskrit K and KH
in Chinese. Asia Major, 1965:199-210.

***

See also 66, 84 - 87, 8 113, 115, 405. Chinese-Sanskrit,
see 639.

Modern Indic languages (in general)

Romanization

104
HARKNESS, H. Ancient and modern alphabets of the popular
Hindu languages of the Southern Peninsula of India. London,
Royal Asiatic Society, 1837.
   Several tables of alphabets using the Devanagari script or
   its derivatives, with Romanization.

105
MONIER WILLIAMS, Sir M. Original papers illustrating the
history of the application of the Roman alphabet to the languages of India. London, Longmans, 1859.

106
WILSON, H.H. A key to professor H.H. Wilson's system of
transliteration. Calcutta, Asiatic Society of Bengal, 1868.

107
MONIER WILLIAMS, Sir M. The duty of English-speaking Orientalists in regard to United Action in adhering generally to
Sir William Jones's Principles of Transliteration, especially
in the Case of Indian Languages; with a proposal for promoting
a Uniform International Method of Transliteration so far at
least as may be applicable to proper names. J. Roy. Asiat.
Soc., 1890:607-629.
   An historic survey of the question from 1780 to the late

1880'ies. Deals with the Devanagari, Greek and Latin alphabets, and proposes a uniform transliteration scheme. The paper was criticized by Sir George A. Grierson, to which Sir Monier Williams replied (p. 814-821 of the same volume).

108
BRUGMANN, K. Zur Transcriptionsmisère. [On the vexed question of transcription.] *Indogermanische Forschungen*, 7, 1897: 167-177.

109
KNOWLES, J., and L. GARTHWAITE. Oriental Braille. One alphabet for the blind for all Oriental languages. London, British and Foreign Bible Society, 1902. 59 p.

110
KNOWLES, J. A national alphabet for India. Eastbourne, 1910. 16 p.

111
KNOWLES, J. Our duty to India and Indian illiterates; romanic letters for Indian languages. London, Christian Literature Society for India, 1910. 66 p.

111a
KNOWLES, J. A common alphabet for Indian languages; or, 53 alphabetic letters for 20,000 syllabic symbols. Eastbourne, W.H. Christian, 1913. 26 p.

112
CHATTERJI, S.K. A Roman alphabet for India. Calcutta, University of Calcutta, 1935. 58 p.

113
SOMMER, F.E. Indic transliteration. *Library J.*, 65, Dec. 1, 1940:990.
  On the discrepancies in transliteration of Sanskrit and other Indic titles or authors, and how these could be avoided if libraries would use the same authorities.

114
JONES, D. The problem of a national script for India. Hertford, Austin, 1942.

115
SITADEVI, A. Language: barrier or bridge, a supplement. *The Adyar Library Bulletin*, 16, 1952:12-22.
  Proposes a new transliteration system without diacritical marks. Examples of application to Hindi, Tamil, French, English and Sanskrit.

116
CHATTERJI, S.K. Phonetic transcriptions in Indian languages. *In* [Festschr. Taraporewala].

117
INDIA. MINISTRY OF EDUCATION. A standard system of Roman transliteration. New Delhi, 1958 9 p. (*Its* Publ. no. 259)

118
RAY, P.S. Romanization in India. Chapter 8 of Language standardization [C], 1963, p.92-105.

119
SENGUPTA, B. Rendering of Indic names-of-person in catalogue entries. In International conference on cataloguing principles, Paris, 1961. London, IFLA, 1963. p. 255-265.

120
LIBRARY OF CONGRESS. Transliteration; languages of India and Pakistan. Cataloging Service, Bulletin 64, Feb. 1964. 21 p.
    Supersedes the transliteration scheme published in Bulletin 31, 1954. 12 Indic languages are covered, viz. Assamese, Bengali, Gujarati, Hindi, Kannada, Malayalam, Marathi, Oriya, Panjabi, Sanskrit, Tamil and Telugu. See also individual entries for these languages.

121
KHERA, K.L. Nagari adjusting to automation. Indian Librarian, 25, Dec. 1970:155-158.
    A scheme for automatic conversion of Devanagari characters into Roman characters is outlined.

122
PATIL, G.M. Reader orientation & transliterating. Dharwar, 1970. vii, 80 p.
    On the Devanagari and Kannada scripts, their use in library catalogs and the problems of their transcription.

Indic languages and Arabic script (general)

123
MAHDIHASSAN, S. A comparative study of Devanagri and Arabic characters. In [Festschr. Gode], 1960. p. 236-259.

124
GOREKAR, N.S. Indian vernaculars in the Arabico-Persian script. Indica, 2, 1965:35-46.

Romanization of individual Indic languages

Assamese

125
LIBRARY OF CONGRESS. [Transliteration of] Assamese. Cataloging Service, Bull. 64, Feb. 1964. p. 2.

Bengali

126
LIBRARY OF CONGRESS. [Transliteration of] Bengali. Cataloging Service, Bull. 64, Feb. 1964. p. 3.

127
ABDUL HUQ, A.M. A study of Bengali Muslim personal names to ascertain the feasibility of application of a mechanistic rule

for their arrangement. Pittsburgh, University of Pittsburgh, 1970. 87 p. (Ph.D. thesis)
　　Transliteration of Bengali names is discussed (p. 51-53).

Gujarati

128
LIBRARY OF CONGRESS. Gujarati. <u>Cataloging Service</u>, Bull. 64, Feb. 1964. p. 4.

Hindi

129
HÄLSIG, M. Zur Transkription und Transliteration des Hindi. [On the transcription and transliteration of Hindi.] Berlin, Institut für Bibliothekswissenschaft der Humboldt-Universität zu Berlin, 1963.

130
LIBRARY OF CONGRESS. Hindi. <u>Cataloging Service</u>, Bulletin 64, Feb. 1964. p. 5-6.

See also 13, 66, 84, 87.

Marathi

131
LIBRARY OF CONGRESS. Marathi. <u>Cataloging Service</u>, Bull. 64, Feb. 1964. p. 9.

Oriya

132
JONES, D. A Romanic orthography for the Oriya language. <u>Zeitschrift für Phonetik und allgemeine Sprachwissenschaft</u>, <u>3</u>, 1949:74-76.

133
LIBRARY OF CONGRESS. Oriya. <u>Cataloging Service</u>, Bull. 64, Feb. 1964. p. 10.

Panjabi

134
LIBRARY OF CONGRESS. Panjabi (Gurmukhi script). <u>Cataloging Service</u>, Bull. 64, Feb. 1964. p. 11.

Sindhi

135
LIBRARY OF CONGRESS. Romanization of Sindhi in Arabic script. <u>Cataloging Service</u>, Bull. 104, April 1972:19-20.

Sinhalese

135a
LIBRARY OF CONGRESS. Sinhalese romanization. <u>Cataloging Service</u>, Bull. 88, Jan. 1970:11.

Place names, see 724.

Urdu

136
LEVA, A.E. Note sugli ultimi sviluppi della scrittura urdu

e sulla sua trascrizione in caratteri latini. [Note on the latest developments of the Urdu script and its transcription into Roman characters.] <u>Oriente Moderno</u>, <u>28</u>, 1948:192-195.

137
MOID, A. Urdu language collections in American libraries. Urbana, Ill., University of Illinois, 1964. 278 l. (Ph.D. thesis)
   Transliteration of the Urdu alphabet, p. 70-75, with tables of comparison between various proposed schemes.

138
LIBRARY OF CONGRESS. Urdu in Arabic script: Romanization. <u>Cataloging Service</u>, Bull. 94, Sept. 1970. 7 p.
   Supersedes earlier scheme, published in Bull. 64, 1964.

***

On modern Indic languages, see also 81, 391-416.
Place names, see 711 - 713.

Kurdish

139
EDMONDS, C.J. Suggestions for the use of Latin characters in the writing of Kurdish. <u>J. Roy. Asiat. Soc.</u>, 1931:27-46.
   Table of transliteration from modified Arabic script (as introduced by Tewfiq Bey) into Roman characters.

140
MINORSKY, V.F. Remarks on the Romanized Kurdish alphabet. <u>J. Roy. Asiat. Soc.</u>, 1933:643-650.
   Supports Edmonds' suggestions and proposes a few improvements. Both Edmonds and Minorsky emphasize the fact that the Arabic script is entirely unsuitable for writing Kurdish.

Old and Middle Iranian (Avestan, Pahlavi)

141
JACKSON, A.V.W. The Avestan alphabet and its transcription. Stuttgart, Kohlhammer, 1890. 36 p.

142
MACKENZIE, D.N. Notes on the transcription of Pahlavi. <u>Bull. Amer. Sch. Orient. Res.</u>, <u>30</u>, 1967, pt. 1:17-29.

New Iranian (Persian)

Romanization

143
BRITISH ACADEMY. Transliteration of Arabic and Persian ... London, 1918. Reprinted from <u>Proc. Brit. Acad.</u>, 1917-18: 505-521.

144
SHARIFY, N. Cataloging of Persian works: including rules for transliteration, entry and description. Chicago, American Library Association, 1959. 161 p. (Ph.D. thesis)

145
LAZARD, G. A proposal for the transliteration of Persian. J. of the Regional Cultural Institute (Iran, Pakistan, Turkey), I/4, 1968:40-42.

146
SOCIETY FOR THE DEVELOPMENT OF THE PERSIAN LANGUAGE. A proposal for the transcription of Persian. J. of the Regional Cultural Institute (Iran, Pakistan, Turkey), I/4, 1968:43-44.

147
LIBRARY OF CONGRESS. Persian romanization. Cataloging Service, Bull. 92, Sept. 1970. 5 p.
    Supersedes earlier scheme, published in Bull. 59, 1963.

Persian-German

148
BRAUN, H. Die alphabetische Katalogisierung von Werken in arabischer, persischer und türkischer Sprache. [The alphabetical cataloging of works in Arabic, Persian and Turkish.] Z. Bibl. Bibliogr., 11, Nr. 1, 1964:9-32.

***

See also 66, 84, 87, 89, 92, 391-393. Place names 711, 715, 721, 738.

Pushto

149
LIBRARY OF CONGRESS. Pushto romanization. Cataloging Service, Bull. 93, Sept. 1970. 5 p.
    Supersedes earlier scheme published in Bull. 71, 1965.

See also 66, 84, 711.

Armenian
Romanization

150
LIBRARY OF CONGRESS. Transliteration. Armenian. Cataloging Service, Bull. 47, Sept. 1958. 1 p.

151
SCHÜTZ, E. On the transcription of Armeno-Kipchak. Acta Orient. Acad. Sci. Hungar., 12, 1961:139-161.

152
MOLNÁR, N. Az örmény és gruz cimek átirásáról. [On the transliteration of Armenian and Georgian entries.] Magyar Könyvszemle, 80, 1964:181-183.

See also 66, 84, 87, 89.

Cyrillization

153
VARTAPETJAN, N.A. [Handbook on Russian transcription of Armenian personal names and place names.] Erevan, Armjanskoe Gos. Izd., 1961. 129 p. (In Russian)

Albanian

154
KRISTOFORID, K. Alfabět škïp. [Albanian alphabet.] Konstantinopol, 1872. 30 p.
  Published earlier (1867?) in an edition printed in Greek letters. Comparison with Greek, Cyrillic, Roman and Arabic.

155
GEITLER, L. Die albanesischen und slavischen Schriften. [The Albanian and Slavic scripts.] Wien, 1883. x, 188 p.

Greek

Romanization

156
BACON, R. The Opus Majus ... edited, with introd. and analytical table, by J.H. Bridges. Oxford, 1897-1900. 3 v.
  "Linguarum cognitio", vol. i, p. 74-77, and in Supplementary vol., p. 89-94. Transliteration table for Greek on p. 75. The frontispiece is a facsimile of MS Vatican 4086, f. 15b, 16a, showing the transliteration table for Hebrew and Greek. One of the earliest attempts at a systematic transliteration of Greek into Latin.

157
Novum instrumentum omne, diligenter ab Erasmo Rot. recognitum et emendatum. [The new instrument (i.e. testament), carefully reviewed and corrected by Erasmus of Rot(terdam).] Basileae, apud Frobenius, 1516.
  The first edition of Erasmus' Latin translation of the N.T. had the word "instrumentum" in its title, which was changed to "testamentum" in the second edition, 1518. The translation, printed in two parallel columns, Greek and Latin, became a kind of standard for the transliteration of Greek during four centuries. The Austrian cataloging rules of 1901 (see 84) refer specifically to "Erasmic transcription".

158
BUCHANAN, R.E. Transliteration of Greek and Latin in the formation of names of zoological taxa. Systematic Zoology, 5, 1956:65-67.
  In theory, names should be transliterated as in classical Latin, following Linnaeus' dictum "The equivalents used by the Romans from all time must be adopted in representing Greek letters"; but in practice, there are many possible variations, due to errors and ambiguities.

159
FENNAH, R.G. Transliteration of Greek words. Systematic Zoology, 6, 1957:194.
  Further on the same subject, and on errors and omissions in the "Rules of Zoological Nomenclature".

160
BRITISH STANDARDS INSTITUTION. British standard for transliteration of Cyrillic and Greek characters. London, 1958. (B.S. 2979:1958)
    The transliteration table for Greek is neither for ancient nor for modern Greek, but tries to strike a "neutral" balance between the two.

161
WALSAS, M. De l'écriture du grec en caractères latins aux XVIe et XVIIe siècles. [On the writing of Greek in Roman characters in the 16th and 17th century.] In Probleme der neugriechischen Literatur [C], Bd. 2, p. 37-39.

162
PRING, J.T. The Romanization of Greek. Le Maître Phonétique, 1960, no. 113:1-4.

163
LECLERCQ, H. Note concernant la translittération en caractères latins des noms de personne attestés par les sources grecques. [Note on the transliteration into Roman characters of personal names documented by Greek sources.] Orbis, 13, 1964:299-308.

164
ROLOFF, H. Die internationale Vereinheitlichung der Transliteration der griechischen Schrift. [The international unification of the transliteration of Greek script.] Zentralbl. Bibliothekswesen, 78, 1964:600-603.
    On the draft proposal for an international standard (see below 165). A critical reply was published in 1966:

164a
DITTEN, H. Bemerkungen zu dem Bericht von Heinrich Roloff "Die Internationale Vereinheitlichung der Transliteration der griechischen Schrift". [Remarks on the report by Heinrich Roloff.] Zentralbl. Bibliothekswesen, 80, 1966:468-473.

165
INTERNATIONAL ORGANIZATION FOR STANDARDIZATION. International system for the transliteration of Greek characters into Latin characters. Geneva, 1968. 7p. (ISO/R 843)
    Identical with B.S. 2979 (see 160).

166
LIBRARY OF CONGRESS. Greek romanization. Cataloging Service, Bull. 104, April 1972, p. 17-18.
    Supersedes table in ALA Cataloging rules (see 90). Includes notes on variations in transliteration from modern Greek, and eliminates some diacritical marks.

Greek-Spanish

167
FERNÁNDEZ-GALIANO, M. La transcripción castellana de los nombres proprios griegos. [The Spanish transcription of Greek proper names.] Madrid, Sociedad Española de Estudios Clásicos, 1961. 144 p.

168
FERNÁNDEZ-GALIANO, M. Sobre la transliteración del griego y el ruso. [On the transliteration of Greek and Russian.] Filología Moderna, 31-32, 1968:277-292.

Greek-German

169
DITTEN, H. Zur Transkription und Transliteration des Griechischen. [On the transcription and transliteration of Greek.] Zentralbl. Bibliothekswesen, 74, Sept. 1960:337-346.

Greek-Bulgarian

170
FILIPOVA-BAJROVA, M. [Pronunciation and transcription of Greek names in Bulgarian.] Bălgarski Ezik, 14, 1964:195-201. (In Bulgarian)

171
BATAKLIEV, G. [Pronunciation and transcription of ancient Greek names in Bulgarian.] Bălgarski Ezik, 17, 1967:543-550. (In Bulgarian)

Greek-Georgian

172
BLAKE, R.P. Greek script and Georgian scribes on Mt. Sinai. Harvard Theological Review, 25, July 1932:273-276.
   On manuscripts of the Gospels written in Greek by Georgian monks who sometimes inserted Georgian letters when transcribing names.

***

See also 84, 86, 87, 88, 89, 90, 390. Hebrew-Greek 419, Arabic-Greek 419, Place names 714.

Latin

173
COSTA, T. Minule propui latineștî in romînește. [Latin proper names in Romanian.] Limba Romînă, 7, no. 4, 1958: 70-77.
   Latin names cannot always be transcribed in their original spelling, because some are known in a "Roumanized" form, others are partially changed. Similar problems arise for Greek names.

Greek-Latin 156, 157, 158. Czech-Latin 279. Turkish-Latin 510-512, 509, 510. Chinese-Latin 577.

ROMANCE LANGUAGES

Spanish

Cyrillization

174
PAHOV, P. [Pronunciation and transcription of Spanish names in Bulgarian.] Bălgarski Ezik, 14, 1964:402-410. (In Bulgarian)

175
TOMOV, T.S. [On the pronunciation and transcription of Portuguese and Spanish proper names in Bulgarian.] Bălgarski Ezik, 15, 1965:383-389. (In Bulgarian)

176
TUROVER, G. JA. [The Russian transcription of Spanish proper names.] Tetradi Perevodčika, 2, 1964:108-120. (In Russian)

***

See also 94. Greek-Spanish 167, 168. Cyrillization of names 388. Chinese-Spanish 640.

Ladino

177
FOULCHÉ-DELBOSC, R. La transcription hispano-hébraique. [The Spanish-Hebrew transcription.] Revue Hispanique, 1, 1894:22-33.
   Deals with the typography of Ladino and some transcription problems.

178
CIROT, G. "Ladino" et "aljamiado". ["Ladino" and "Aljamiado".] Bulletin Hispanique, 38, 1936:538-540.
   Spanish written in Hebrew characters (Ladino) and Spanish written in Arabic characters (Aljamiado).

179
MILLÁS-VALLICROSA, J.M. Sobre una moderna dejación de la escritura aljamiada hebraico-española. [On a modern relinquishment of the Ladino script.] Sefarad, 10, 1950:185-186.
   After the Latinization of Turkish, Sephardic Jews in Turkey begin to Romanize Ladino. Passages from a Romanized Haggada are quoted as examples.

180
RENARD, R. L'influence du mode de transcription sur le système phonique du judéo-espagnol. [The influence of the mode of transcription on the phonic system of Ladino.] Revue de Phonétique Appliquée, 2, 1966:35-40.

Judeo-Arabic

181
MILLÁS-VALLICROSA, J.M. and BUSQUETS MULET, J. Albaranes mallorquines en aljamiado hebraicoárabe. [Mallorcan hand-

written signs in Judeo-Arabic script.] <u>Sefarad</u>, <u>4</u>, 1944: 275-286.

182
BOSCH VILÁ, J. Escrituras oscenses en aljámia hebraico-árabe. [Oscanian inscriptions in Judeo-Arabic.] [Festschr. Millás-Vallicrosa] 1954:183-214.

***

Hebrew-Judeo=Arabic 447.

Portuguese

Cyrillic-Portuguese 239, 239a. Cyrillization of names 388. Arabic-Portuguese 485.

French
Arabization

183
BOURGEOIS, H. La transcription arabe du français. <u>Revue du Monde Musulman</u>, <u>40-41</u>, 1920:157-164.

***

See also 95, 115. Cyrillic-French 240. Cyrillization of names 355, 388. Arabic-French 486-488. Chinese-French 600, 641, 642.

Italian
Hebraization

184
TREVES, M. I termini italiani di Donnolo e di Assaf (sec. X). [The Italian terms of Donnolo and Assaf (10th century)]. <u>Lingua</u>, <u>22</u>, 1961:64-66.
  The transliteration of Latin and Italian botanical and pharmaceutical terms in the works of the Jewish physicians Donnolo and Assaf, written in Hebrew.

***

Cyrillization of names 388. Arabic-Italian 489.

Romanian

185
SACERDOŢEANU, A. Ceva despre transcrierea documentelor româneşti. [Something about the transcription of documents into Romanian.] <u>Revista Arhivelor</u>, <u>3</u>, 1939:283-312.

***

Romanian in Cyrillic characters ("Alfabetul cirilic") 87, 88, 226. Latin-Romanian 173. Cyrillic-Romanian 240a, 241. Serbo=Croatian-Romanian 277. Czech-Romanian 280. Cyrillization of names 388. Chinese-Romanian 643, 644. Place names 707.

GAELIC

186
BRITISH MUSEUM. DEPARTMENT OF PRINTED BOOKS. Rules for compiling the catalogue of printed books, maps and music in the British Museum. London, 1936.
    Transliteration of Gaelic names, p. 50.

187
BIBLIOTECA APOSTOLICA VATICANA. Norme per il catalogo degli stampati. Roma, 1939.
    Has a table of transcription for Gaelic, p. 459.

GERMANIC LANGUAGES

German

Cyrillization

188
TISCHNER, J.K. Wechselseitige Umschreibung fremder Eigennamen im deutschen und slawischen Schrifttum; für Autoren, Buchdrucker ... [Reciprocal transcription of foreign proper names in the German and Slavic literature; for authors, printers, etc.] Berlin, Bildungsverband der deutschen Buchdrucker, 1930. 40 p.

189
DOLGOPOL'SKIJ, A.B. [The transcription of German *ai*, *ei*, *eu*.] Voprosi kul'turi reči, 6, 1965:163-165. (In Russian)

190
MULISCH, H. Zur Transkription deutscher Eigennamen bei Uebersetzungen ins Russische. [On the transcription of German proper names in translation into Russian.] Fremdsprachenunterricht, 10, 1966:412-416.

191
ŠEVOROŠKIN, V.V. [On the transliteration of German diphthongs.] In Slavjanskaja leksikografia [C], 1966. p. 140-141. (In Russian)

192
ZIKMUND, H. Die deutschen I-Diphthonge in russischer Schreibung und Lautung. [The German I-diphthongs in Russian spelling and pronunciation.] Forschungen und Fortschritte, 40, 1966:153-155.

Hebraization

193
GUGGENHEIM-GRÜNBERG, F. Ein deutscher Urfehdebrief in hebräischer Schrift aus Zürich vom Jahre 1385. [A German oath-of-truce in Hebrew script from Zurich, dated 1385.] Z. Mundartforschung, 22, 1954:207-214.
    A phonetic transliteration from late medieval Swiss-German in Hebrew letters, intended for the use of Gentiles. Gives valuable clues to the actual pronunciation of this German dialect in the 14th century.

194
PAPER, H.H. An early case of standard German in Hebrew orthography. In The field of Yiddish [C], 1954. p. 143-146.
   A translation of Baḥya ibn Paquda's work "Ḥovot halevavot" into Yiddish and into High German (the first chapter only) by Moses Steinhard (Fürth, 1765). The German translation is written in Hebrew characters in rabbinic script.

195
GUGGENHEIM-GRÜNBERG, F. Zur Umschrift deutscher Mundarten des 14./15. Jahrhunderts mit hebräischer Schrift. [On the transcription of German dialects of the 14th and 15th century in Hebrew script.] Z. Mundartforschung, 24, 1956:229-246.
   Two legal documents, one from Frankfurt a.M., the other from Breslau, in Hebrew transliteration which tries to give the pronunciation rather than the actual German spelling. The German text of the documents is also preserved which allows for comparison.

***

See also 28, 84, 87, 92, 95. Persian-German 143. Greek-German 169. Cyrillic-German 242-257. Russian-German 332-359. Cyrillization of names 355, 388. Hebrew-German 426a. Arabic-German 490. Turkish-German 490, 513. Japanese-German 563-566, 646. Chinese-German 645. Place names 709, 717-720, 739.

Yiddish

Romanization

196
BIRNBAUM, S.A. Praktische Grammatik der jiddischen Sprache für den Selbstunterricht ... [Practical grammar of the Yiddish language for self-study.] Wien, A. Hartleben, 1915.
   Transliteration table, p. 11-15.
   A 2nd ed. was published by Buske, Hamburg, 1966.

196a
BIRNBAUM, S.A. [Transcriptions of Yiddish] Filologishe Shriftn [fun YIWO], 2, 1929:485-496. (In Yiddish)

197
BIRNBAUM, S.A. Umschrift des ältesten datierten jiddischen Schriftstücks. [Transcription of the oldest dated Yiddish document.] Teuthonista, 8, 1931/32:197-207.
   A text-critical edition of the Yiddish translation of a 14th century German medical treatise. There are two tables of transliteration: Yiddish-Roman (for the text itself) and Romanized Yiddish-German.

198
BIRNBAUM, S.A. Die Umschrift des Jiddischen. [The Romanization of Yiddish.] Teuthonista, 9, 1933:90-105.
   Based on his earlier research (196-197), the author proposes a scientifically correct Romanization scheme.

199
WEINREICH, U. Note on transcription, transliteration, and citation of titles. In The field of Yiddish [C], 1954. Preface, p. vi-viii.
> Modern Yiddish (after 1800) is transliterated by the YIWO system (a phonemic system). Pre-1800 Yiddish is transliterated by a letter-by-letter system because the exact pronunciation is not always known.

199a
WEINREICH, U. Modern English-Yiddish, Yiddish-English dictionary. New York, McGraw-Hill and YIWO Institute for Jewish Research, 1968. 1 v.
> Yiddish-English transcription table on p. xxiv-xxv.

***

See also 89, 193-195, 421.

Dutch

Czech and Polish-Dutch 281, Russian-Dutch 360, 361, Cyrillization 388, Chinese-Dutch 647, 648.

English

Cyrillization

200
IIVAINEN, L. The rendering of English proper names in Russian. Slavonic and East European Review, 39, Dec. 1960: 137-147.

201
KUZNECOVA, V.I. [Phonetic fundamentals of rendering English proper names in the Russian language.] Leningrad, Učpedgiz, 1960. 119 p. (In Russian)

201a
GRAMENZ, F.T., and KIPARSKY, V. Englische und pseudoenglische Namen bei russischen Schriftstellern. [English and pseudo-English names used by Russian writers.] Wiesbaden, Harrassowitz, 1961.
> Explores the methods by which English names (real and fictitious) are transcribed by various Russian authors. Table of Russian-English sound equivalents, p. 2.

***

Cyrillization of names 355, 388. Place names 740, 741.

Transcription into Chinese

202
HSIN, HUA. [Handbook of English names, transcribed into Chinese.] Peking, 1965. iv, 381 p. (In Chinese)

***

See also 95, 115.

Danish

Cyrillic-Danish 257a, Russian-Danish 361a.

Swedish
Cyrillization

203
DURIDANOV, I. [Pronunciation and transcription of Swedish names in Bulgarian.] Bălgarski Ezik, 17, 1967:242-247. (In Bulgarian)

See also 388. Cyrillic-Swedish 258, 259, 259a.

BALTIC LANGUAGES

Lithuanian

204
PAULAUSKS, J. Norādījumi par lietuviešu valodas īpašvārdu atdarināšanu latviešu valodā. [Notes on the transcription of Lithuanian place names and personal names into Latvian.] Latvijas Padomju Socialistikas Republikas Zinatnu Akademija, no. 5, 1962:148-150.

Hebrew-Lithuanian 445.

SLAVIC LANGUAGES

Romanization

205
BRITISH ACADEMY. Transliteration of Slavonic. Report of the Committee appointed to draw up a practical scheme for the transliteration into English of words and names belonging to Russian and other Slavonic languages. Proc. Brit. Acad., 8, 1917-18:523-542.
    Table of transliteration for printed and written (italic) Cyrillic characters, without the use of any diacritics.

206
KERNER, R.J. Slavic Europe: a selected bibliography in the Western European languages. Cambridge, Harvard University Press, 1918. xxiv, 402 p.
    Has notes on the theory of transliteration, and a transliteration table for Russian and Bulgarian, following the Library of Congress scheme with minor variations.

207
Pronunciation of Slavonic words and names. Slavonic Review, 2, March 1924:668-672.
    Compares Slavic names as spelled in the Cyrillic and Roman alphabets.

208
DAMIANI, E. Sull' unificazione della trascrizione dei nomi slavi, originariamente scritti in caratteri cirillici nel cataloghi delle biblioteche a caratteri latini. [On the unification of the translation of Slavic names, originally written in Cyrillic characters, in library catalogs using Roman characters.] L'Europa Orientale, 1935.

209
DAMIANI, E. Sulla questione della trascrizione dei caratteri cirillici in caratteri latini e viceversa. [On the question of transcription of Cyrillic characters into Roman characters and vice versa.] Rivista Italo-Bulgara di Letteratura, Storia, Arte, 6, 1936:392-393.

210
DAMIANI, E. Ancora sulla trascrizione dei nomi cirillici in caratteri latini sotto l'aspetto biblioteconomico e bibliografico. [Again on the transcription of Cyrillic names in Roman characters from the point of view of library management and bibliography.] Revue Internationale des Etudes Balkaniques, 3, 1938:617-623.

211
DAMIANI, E. Sur l'état actuel des systèmes de transcription des noms slaves cyrilliques dans la documentation bibliographique. Trans. Int. Fed. Docum., 14, 1938:245-248.
  This summarizes the author's previous papers (208-210) and compares the system of Croatian transliteration of Serbian (the "international scientific system") with the Soviet scheme and the Library of Congress scheme. The use of the "scientific" system is recommended for libraries and for bibliographical work.

212
DAMIANI, E. Norme adottate e da adottare per l'unificazione bibliografica dei nomi d'autori variamente trascritti de lingue a caratteri diversi dall'alfabeto latino, con particolare riguardo all'alfabeto cirillico. [Standards adopted and to be adopted for the bibliographical unification of authors' names variously transcribed from languages using different scripts into the Roman alphabet, with particular reference to the Cyrillic alphabet.] Accademie e Biblioteche d'Italia, 14, 1940:409-413.

213
Návrh na transliteraci cyrilského písma do latinky. [Proposal for the transliteration of Cyrillic script into Roman.] Slavia, 17, 1939/40:317-320.

214
JONES, M.B. Inclusive and uniform alphabet for Russian, Bulgarian, Serb-Croatian [sic], Czech and Polish. Claremont, Claremont Colleges, 1941. 35 l.
  Roman characters with Czech diacritical marks.

215
TRAGER, G.L. The transliteration of Russian and other Slavic alphabets. Studies in Linguistics, 1, 1942. 4 p.

216
Transliterace cyrilského pisma do latinky. [The transliteration of Cyrillic script into Roman.] Slavia, 20, 1950: 158-161.

217
FRITSCHY, G.J.M. De normalisatie van de translitteratie van Cyrillisch schrift. [The standardization of transliteration of the Cyrillic script.] Biblioteekleven, 37, 1952:293-295.
   Suggests desirability of two systems, one with diacritical marks for scholarly and research libraries, another without such marks, like the one used by Chemical Abstracts, for popular libraries.

218
MATTHEWS, W.K. The Latinization of Cyrillic characters. Slavonic and East European Review, 30, June 1952:531-548.
   A revised version is reprinted in B.S. 2979 (see 226).

219
Transliteration of Cyrillic script. Nature, 171, March 28, 1953:548.
   The anonymous contributor recommends the universal use of the Royal Society scheme. In his reply, M. Aurousseau states (May 23, 1953:940) that this would not be suitable for geographical purposes, and that probably more than one scheme should be used for different purposes.

220
PACLT, J. Transliteration of Cyrillic for use in botanical nomenclature. Taxon, 2, 1953:159-166.
   Recommends use of diacritical marks to preserve the original spelling of names of persons after which plants and animals have been named. Phonetics are here of secondary importance.

221
ROYAL SOCIETY. The transliteration of Russian, Serbian and Bulgarian for bibliographical purposes, prepared by H.S. Bushell. London, 1953. 12 p.
   Cyrillic-English and English-Cyrillic transliteration tables, using a minimum of diacritical marks. The Croatian-Serbian transliteration is also shown in a table.

222
INTERNATIONAL ORGANIZATION FOR STANDARDIZATION. International system for the transliteration of Cyrillic characters. Geneva, 1954. (ISO/R 9)
   The first international transliteration standard. Uses diacritical marks based on the Croatian usage. Superseded by 1968 edition (see 236).

223
KRAL, W. Zu einer internationalen Transliteration der kyrillischen Buchstaben. [On an international transliteration of Cyrillic characters.] Zentralbl. Bibliothekswesen, 69, 1955:343-356.

225
PACLT, J. Randbemerkungen zur internationalen Transliteration der kyrillischen Alphabete. [Remarks on the international transliteration of the Cyrillic alphabets.] <u>Zentralbl. Bibliothekswesen</u>, <u>70</u>, 1956:216-217.

226
BRITISH STANDARDS INSTITUTION. British standard for transliteration of Cyrillic and Greek characters. London, 1958. 23 p. (B.S. 2979:1958)
 Cyrillic-English and English-Cyrillic transliteration tables for Russian, Ukrainian, White-Russian, Bulgarian, Serbian, Macedonian, Church Slavic and Romanian. The scheme follows mainly the joint Royal Society and British Academy scheme with minor variations. The ISO international transliteration scheme is also included as an alternative.

227
ALLEN, C.G. [Review of 226.] <u>Journal of Documentation</u>, <u>15</u>, no. 1, 1959:116-117.

228
PODBORNY, J.G. Zu einer international einheitlichen Umschreibung der kyrillischen Buchstaben. [On an internationally uniform Romanization of Cyrillic characters.] <u>Babel</u>, <u>5</u>, no. 4, Dec. 1959:207-212.

229
GILJAREVSKIJ, R.S. and N.V. KRYLOVA. [Transliteration of bibliographic entries in the languages of the USSR with letters of the Roman alphabet.] <u>Sovetskaja Bibliografija</u>, <u>5</u>, no. 63, 1960:37-44. (In Russian)
 The ISO/R 9 standard, based on the work of the Soviet linguist L.V. Ščerba and a subsequent Soviet scheme, did not include transliterations of the additional characters used in the alphabets of non-Slavic peoples in the USSR. The paper therefore proposes such transliteration tables. Of the 65 officially recognized languages in the USSR, seven (Armenian, Georgian, Yiddish, Latvian, Lithuanian, Finnish and Estonian) do not use the Cyrillic script; 16 (Balkarian, Koryak, Kumy, Mansij, Moldavian, Mordvin-Mokshan, Mordvin-Erzian, Nanaj, Nenec, Nivh Nogaj, Sel'kup, and the languages of the Suryškar Hants, Evenkij, Even and Eskimo) use the regular Cyrillic alphabet; and the remaining 42 languages need more letters. These special letters and their Roman equivalents are tabulated. The system is already used by the Soviet All-Union Book Chamber. French translation in 231.

230
ROYAL SOCIETY. The transliteration of Cyrillic characters into the Roman alphabet. FID 26th international conference, Rio de Janeiro, July 1960. 2 p.

231
La translittération des caractères cyrilliques, à propos de deux articles récents. [The transliteration of Cyrillic characters, apropos of two recent articles.] Bull. Bibl. France, 6, June 1961:278-292.
 A full French translation of 229 and 230.

232
KOTLABA, F., and Z. POUZAR. A proposal on the transliteration of Slavonic authors' names. Taxon, 11, 1962:113-115.

233
RIGBY, J.F., and S. DOBRIANSKIJ. Comments on "A proposal on the transliteration of Slavonic authors' names". Taxon, 11, 1962:214-215.

234
BIDWELL, C.E. Alphabets of the modern Slavic languages. Pittsburgh, Pittsburgh University, 1967. 24 p.
 A short historical introduction to the alphabets of the Czech, Russian, Ukrainian, White-Russian, Bulgarian, Slovenian, Serbo-Croatian, Macedonian and Polish language, and the Church Slavic alphabet, with tables of transliteration and pronunciation. The ISO/R9 scheme is used throughout, except for Cyrillic x which is transliterated x (not h).

235
GAKOVICH, R. The problem of transliteration of Slavic languages. University of Wisconsin Library News, 13, no. 3, 1962:7-12.
 The multiplicity of transliteration systems for Slavic languages makes bibliographical searches difficult. A comparative table of the schemes used by the Library of Congress, ISO, BSI, the Board of Geographic Names and the New York Public Library is presented.

236
INTERNATIONAL ORGANIZATION FOR STANDARDIZATION. International system for the transliteration of Slavic Cyrillic characters. 2nd ed. Geneva, 1968. 8 p. (ISO/R9)
 The main difference between this and the first edition is the optional inclusion of alternative "English" transliterations of those Cyrillic letters which are rendered with the aid of diacritical marks in the basic scheme; these may be transliterated by digraphs, e.g. Ш may be written by sh instead of š, Ж by zh instead of ž, etc.

237
INTERNATIONAL ATOMIC ENERGY AGENCY. Transliteration rules for selected non-Roman characters. Vienna, 1970. 7 p. (IAEA-INIS-10)
 Transliteration tables for the Cyrillic and Greek alphabet, mainly following ISO/R 9, with minor variations.

238
VILDÉ-LOT, I. La nouvelle édition de la recommendation ISO/R9 pour la translitération des caractères cyrilliques. [The new edition of Recommendation ISO/R9 for the transliteration of Cyrillic characters.] Bull. Bibl. France, 15, Dec. 1970:609-613.
  The changes in the 2nd ed. are examined and difficulties are foreseen if libraries and union catalogs adopt the revisions. There is a pressing need to reconcile the ISO and the Anglo-Saxon systems.

***

See also 15, 23, 32, 66, 77, 86, 88, 89, 90, 96, 155, 386, and under each Slavic language.

Cyrillic-Portuguese

239
ASSOCIAÇÃO BRASILEIRA DE NORMAS TÉCNICAS. Transliteração de caracteres cirílicos. [Transliteration of Cyrillic characters.] Boletim da Associaçao Brasileira de Normas Técnicas, 8, set./oct. 1961:13-16. (P-NB-102)

Cyrillic-French

240
UNION FRANÇAISE DES ORGANISMES DE DOCUMENTATION. Transcription des caractères cyrilliques. [Transcription of Cyrillic characters.] Documentation en France, 8, June 1939:18.
  A comparative tables of the systems proposed by the International Standards Association (the later ISO) and UFOD.

241
ASSOCIATION FRANÇAISE DE NORMALISATION. Translittération des caractères cyrilliques. [Transliteration of cyrillic characters.] Paris, 1971. (AFNOR Z 46-001)
  The official French standard, revised according to ISO/R9 2nd ed., 1968. An earlier version, also strictly according to ISO/R9, was published in 1956.

Cyrillic-Romanian

242
VIRTOSU, E. Transcrierea textelor chirilice romînești. [Transcription of Cyrillic Romanian texts.] Studii Teologice, 15, no. 1-2, 1963:65-104.
  A history of Romanian texts in the Cyrillic script (mainly of a religious nature), and how to transcribe these into modern Romanian.

Cyrillic-German

243
KOSCHMIDER, E. Zur Transkription der Slavika. [On the transcription of Slavic works.] Zentralbl. Bibliothekswesen, 46, 1929:615-617.

244
TISCHNER, J.K. Wechselseitige Umschreibung fremder Eigennamen im deutschen und slawischen Schrifttum; für Autoren,

Buchdrucker ... [Reciprocal transcription of foreign proper names in the German and Slavic literature; for authors, printers, etc.] Berlin, Bildungsverband der deutschen Buchdrucker, 1930. 40 p.

245
MACH, O. Die Transkription der kyrillischen Schrift. [The transcription of the Cyrillic script.] Berlin, 1944. (Thesis)

246
SCHUCHMANN, M. Transliteration kyrillischer Buchstaben. Mit Normblattentwurf. [Transliteration of Cyrillic characters; with a draft standard.] Nachrichten für Dokumentation, 5, 1954:46-48.

247
BARNDT, G. Die Transliteration und Transkription kyrillischer Schriftzeichen bei der Dokumentation sowjetischen Schrifttums. [The transliteration and transcription of Cyrillic characters in the documentation of Soviet literature.] Dokumentation, 5, 1958:46.

248
ELSNER, H.A. Uebertragung kyrillischer Buchstaben in lateinische (Transkription und Transliteration). [Romanization of Cyrillic characters (transcription and transliteration.] Arbeitsblätter für betriebliches Informationswesen, ABI 14, 1959. 4 p.

249
BRAUNE, G. Zur Transliteration der kyrillischen Schriftzeichen. [On the transliteration of Cyrillic characters.] Die Bergakademie, 12, 1960:627-629.

250
RECK, H.F. Die Umschreibung (Transkription) ausländischer Personennamen im inländischen Verwaltungsverkehr. [The Romanization (transcription) of foreign personal names in internal administrative practice.] Verwaltung, 13, 1960:331-337.

251
RICHTER, Erich. Zur Transliteration der kyrillischen Buchstaben des russischen Alphabets. [On the transliteration of the Cyrillic characters of the Russian alphabet.] Börsenbl. Deut. Buchhandel, 16, 1960:1332-1337.

252
RECK, H.F. Zur Umschreibung von Eigennamen aus den kyrillisch geschriebenen slawischen Sprachen in der deutschen Presse und Literatur. [On the Romanization of proper names from Slavic languages written in Cyrillic script in the German press and literature.] Osteuropa, 11, 1961:179-188.

253
DEUTSCHER NORMENAUSSCHUSS. Transliteration slawischer kyrillischer Buchstaben. [Transliteration of Slavic Cyrillic characters.] Berlin, 1962. (DIN 1460)

The German standard conforms with ISO/R9, except for Cyrillic x which is transliterated ch, following long-standing German practice. Covers Bulgarian, Russian, Ukrainian, White-Russian and Serbian.

254
HOCHSTEIN, I. Transliteration slawischer kyrillischer Buchstaben. [Transliteration of Slavic Cyrillic characters.] DIN-Mitteilungen, 41, Nr. 10, 1962:461-463.

255
RICHTER, Erich. Zur Transliteration der zusätzlichen Buchstaben in den Alphabeten der Völker der Sowjetunion mit kyrillischer Schrift. [On the transliteration of the additional letters in the alphabets of peoples of the Soviet Union using Cyrillic script.] Dokumentation, Fachbibliothek, Werksbücherei, 10, 1961-62:128-133.

256
RICHTER, Erich. Zur Norm DIN 1460 "Transliteration slawischer kyrillischer Buchstaben". [On the German Standard DIN 1460 "Transliteration of Slavic Cyrillic characters".] Z. Bibl. Bibliogr., 11, Nr. 1, 1964:1-8.

257
SMOLIK, W. Zur Transliteration kyrillischer Buchstaben. [On the transliteration of Cyrillic characters.] ZIID-Zeitschrift, 12, 1965:139-141.

Cyrillic-Swedish

258
KJELLBERG, L. De svenska vetenskapliga bibliotekens translitterering av cyrillisk skrift. [Transliteration of Cyrillic script in Swedish research libraries.] Nordisk Tidskrift för Bok- och Biblioteksväsen, 36, nr. 4, 1949:175-189.
English summary on p. 189.

259
KJELLBERG, L. Slavistik för bibliotekarier. [Slavic languages for librarians.] Lund, Bibliotekstjänst, 1963. 76 p.
Gives tables of two transliteration schemes: the one used in research libraries (see below, item 259a), and one used in smaller public libraries which is modeled on the transliteration scheme used in the Swedish popular encyclopedia Nordisk familjebok (2;a uppl., bd. 23, sp. 1372).

259a
SWEDEN. SVERIGES STANDARDISERINGSKOMMISSION. Translitterering av kyrilliska bokstäver. [Transliteration of Cyrillic characters.] Stockholm, 1963. (SIS 01 10 21)
The official Swedish transliteration standard for Cyrillic, identical with ISO/R9.

Cyrillic-Polish

260
HORODYSKI, B. O transliteracji druków cyrylickich. [On the transliteration of Cyrillic texts.] Przegląd Biblioteczny, 16, no. 3-4. 1948: 171-179.

261
POLSKI KOMITET NORMALIZACYJNY. Transliteracja alfabetów cyrylickich. [Transliteration of Cyrillic alphabets.] Warszawa, 1960. (PN/59/N-01201)
 The Polish transliteration standard follows ISO/R9.

262
KLIMASZEWSKA, K. Transkrypcja czy transliteracja. [Transcription or transliteration.] Aktualne Problemy Informacji i Dokumentacji, 10, no.5, 1965:5-7.
 The problem of transliteration and/or transcription in Poland and on the international level is discussed. The scope of both methods, the difficulties that arise in their use and the possibility of re-transliteration are explored. The conclusion is drawn that transliteration is better suited for documentation purposes. See also 264.

263
KLIMASZEWSKA, K. Transkrypcja czy transliteracja. Warszawa, CIINTE, 1966. (Prace studia przyczynki, no. 3)
 A more detailed version of 262.

264
BROCKI, Z., and J. WIKSEL. Transkrypcja czy transliteracja; wypowiędzi czytelników. [Transcription or transliteration; comments by readers.] Aktualne Problemy Informacji i Dokumentacji, 11, no. 5, 1966:18-20.
 A rejoinder to 262.

265
KLIMASZEWSKA, K. Transkrypcja i transliteracja alfabetów cyrylickich w śnietle ankiety przeprowadzonej w ośrodkach informacji. [Transcription or transliteration of Cyrillic alphabets: results of a poll at the information center.] Aktualne Problemy Informacji i Dokumentacji, 13, no. 2, 1968:5-8.
 A poll about the usefulness of transliteration or transcription in retrieving Cyrillic documents at the Polish Scientific Information Center gave the following results: 41% preferred transcription, 37% preferred transliteration, and 22% found both methods equally useful.

266
CHOROSZUSZYNA, J. Transliteracja, ale jaka? [Transliteration - yes, but which one?] Aktualne Problemy Informacji i Dokumentacji, 11, no. 1, 1966:8-14.
 Several national transliteration systems are compared with ISO/R9. A revision of the transliteration rules seems to be necessary for the sake of logical consistency as well as for practical considerations.

Cyrillic-Hungarian

267
KNIESZA, I. Cirillbetűs szláv szövegek nemzetközi tudományos átírása. [Cyrillic script of Slavic texts in general

scientific transcription.] *Magyar Könyvszemle*, 63, no. 2, 1939:149-158.
 The history and development of the Cyrillic alphabets of Slavic languages. Discussion of the transliteration system used by the Széchenyi Library of the Hungarian National Muesum in Budapest.

268
DESZÖ, L. A cirillbetűs címek átírásának néhány kérdése. [Some problems of the transliteration of titles in Cyrillic characters.] *Magyar Könyvszemle*, 77, April 1961:198-203.

269
MOLNÁR, N. Adalékok a nem szláv cirillbetűs szavak címátírásához. [Contributions to the transliteration of non-Slavic words in Cyrillic characters.] *Magyar Könyvszemle*, 77, April 1961:196-198.

270
RADÓ, G. A Szovjetunió nyelveinek átírási kérdéseihez. [On the question of transliteration of the languages of the Soviet Union.] *Magyar Könyvszemle*, 78, 1962:93-96.

271
DESZÖ, L. A cirillbetűs címek nemzetközi átírása. [Transcription of titles in the Cyrillic alphabet.] *Magyar Könyvszemle*, 79, July 1963:217-273.

Church Slavic (Glagolitic script)

Romanization

272
LESKIEN, A. Handbuch der altbulgarischen (altkirchenslawischen) Sprache; Grammatik, Texte, Glossar. [Handbook of the Old Bulgarian (Old Church Slavic) language; grammar, texts, glossary.] 6. Aufl. Heidelberg, C. Winter, 1922. xvi, 351 p.
 The ALA Joint Code of 1908 (see 86) cites this work as the authority for transliteration of Church Slavic.

See also 84, 87, 226, 234.

Bulgarian

Romanization

273
ROWLAND, P. Transliteration of Bulgarian. Sofia, American College, 1931. 8 p.

Cyrillization

274
ANDREEV, V.D. [The rendering of Bulgarian proper names in Russian.] In *Toponomastika* [C], 1964. (In Russian)

***

See also 84, 87, 90, 213, 221, 222, 224, 226, 234-236, 253, 259, 261. Greek-Bulgarian 170, 171. Spanish-Bulgarian 174,

175. Portuguese-Bulgarian 175. Swedish-Bulgarian 203. Czech-Bulgarian 282. Slovakian-Bulgarian 287. Russian-Bulgarian 362. Ukrainian-Bulgarian 366. White-Russian-Bulgarian 369. Cyrillization 388. Arabic-Bulgarian 491.

Macedonian

Romanization

275
DESZÖ, L. A fehérorosz és makedón címek átírásáról. [The transliteration of White-Russian and Macedonian titles.] Magyar Könyvszemle, 79, Oct. 1961:520-521.

See also 83, 222, 224, 226, 234, 236, 259, 261, 711.

Serbo-Croatian

Romanization

276
MULJAČIĆ, Ž. Les phonèmes italiens /ĉ/ et /ĝ/ dans les emprunts italiens du serbo-croate: problèmes de transcription et de distance phonématique. [The Italian phonemes /ĉ/ and /ĝ/ in Italian loanwords of Serbo-Croatian: problems of transcription and of phonematic distance.] In [Festschr. Jakobson] 1967, vol. 2:1408-1413.

277
TOMICI, M. [Standards of transcription for Serbo-Croatian words and names into Romanian.] Limba Romînă, 13, no. 6, 1964:565-569. (In Romanian)

Arabization

278
BOURGEOIS, H. La transcription arabe du serbe. [The Arabic transcription of Serbian.] Revue du Monde Musulman, 23, 1913:296-304.

***

See also 83, 84, 90, 213, 221, 222, 224, 226, 234 - 236, 253, 259, 261. Cyrillization of names 388.

Slovenian

See 234.

Czech

Romanization

279
RYBA, B. Komenského pokrový latinský pravopis a návrh na jeho transkripci. [The Latin orthography of Comenius and his proposal for transcription.] Listy Filologické, 73, 1949:241-258.

Czech-Romanian

280
FELIX, J. Cu privire la transcrierea numelor de persoane și a toponimicelor cehe. [Transcription of Czech personal and place names into Romanian.] Limba Romînă, 5, 1956:102-103.

Czech-Dutch

281
THYS, E. Translittereren ofte niet? [To transliterate or not?] Bibliotheeksgids, 29, March-April 1953:30-33.
 On the difficulties of transliterating Czech and Polish words and names, with respect to the use of diacritical marks.

Cyrillization
Czech-Bulgarian

282
IVANČEV, S. [Transcription and pronunciation of Czech names in Bulgarian.] Bălgarski Ezik, 10, 1959:231. (In Bulgarian)

Czech-Russian

283
MEL'NIKOV, E.P. [Notes on the morphology and orthography of Czech proper names in Russian transcription.] In Toponomastika [C], 1964. (In Russian)

284
OLIVERIUS, Z.F. [Transliteration of Czech words in the Russian alphabet.] In Russkij jazyk [C], 1965, p. 4-20. (In Russian)

285
HŘIVNÁČ, J. Přepis českých názvů azbukou. [The transcription of Czech names into the Russian alphabet.] In Sborník prací Pedagogické Fakulty v Ostravě, D 1, 1966:33-46.

Transcription into Czech

286
TRNKA, B. Lidová transkripce cizích jmen. [Popular transcription of foreign names.] Časopis pro moderní filologii, 36, 1954:55-56.

***

See also 32, 213, 234. Cyrillic-Czech 212, 215. Cyrillization 388. Oriental languages-Czech 414a.

Slovakian

Cyrillization

287
IVANČEV, S. [The transcription and pronunciation of Slovakian names in Bulgarian.] Bălgarski Ezik, 17, 1967:352-361.

See also 363, 388.

Polish

Polish-Dutch

288
THYS, E. Translittereren ofte niet? [To transliterate or not?] <u>Bibliotheksgids</u>, <u>29</u>, March-April 1953:30-33.
   On the difficulties of transliterating Czech and Polish words and names, with respect to the use of diacritical marks.

Cyrillization

289
PIRUG, L. [On the question of transliteration of Polish proper names into Russian.] <u>Gdańskie Zeszyty Humanistyczne. 10. Filologia Rosyjska</u>. 1, 1967:107-119. (In Russian)

***

See also 213, 234. Cyrillic-Polish 260-266. Russian-Polish 364. Cyrillization 388. Hebrew-Polish 446. Chinese-Polish 649.

Russian

Latinization

290
New Russian alphabet. <u>Science</u>, n.s. <u>60</u>, Dec. 1924, supplement p. xii.

291
BRAUN, F. Die Latinisierung der russischen Schrift. [The Latinization of the Russian script.] <u>Archiv für Schreib- und Buchwesen</u>, <u>4</u>, 1930:139-144.
   A survey of the movement towards the gradual elimination of the Cyrillic script and the introduction of Roman characters for the Russian language. Reprinted in 22.

292
ŽIRKOV, L. [Is the Roman alphabet applicable to all languages?] <u>Kultura i Pismennost' Vostoka</u>, <u>7-8</u>, 1931:38-57. (In Russian)

293
JOPSON, N.B. Russian transliteration. <u>Slavonic Review</u>, <u>12</u>, April 1934:704-713.
   Recommends his own scheme of Latinization, based on phonetic principles and avoiding diacritical marks, for use in Russia, in view of the movement towards Latinisation.

294
MORISON, W.A. The adaptation of the Latin alphabet to Russian. <u>Slavonic Review</u>, <u>12</u>, Jan. 1934:430-435.
   Offers a new transliteration scheme for use in Russia, also inspired by the movement for Latinisation there. The scheme is designed to be useful for all languages using the Roman alphabet and has no diacritical marks.

See also 28, 518.

Romanization

295
A uniform system of Russian transliteration. **Nature**, **41**, no. 1061, Feb. 27, 1890:396-397.
   A transliteration system worked out by a committee of 16 experts, editors of scientific journals, librarians and directors of museums in the U.K., U.S. and Russia, who pledged themselves to use the system in their publications and collections, so as to achieve maximum uniformity. There is a Russian-English and English-Russian (re-transliteration) table.

295a
BOLTON, H.C. Russian transliteration. **Library J.**, **17**, 1892:383-384.
   A reprint of 295, preceded by a note from Bolton (who was one of the American committee members), urging the adoption of the scheme also by American libraries. Proposes to convene a conference to reconcile the few inconsistencies between the American and the new British system.

296
SMITH, J.S. Transliteration from Russian. **New Englander and Yale Review**, **54**, 1891:431.

297
GREAT BRITAIN. WAR OFFICE. INTELLIGENCE DIVISION. A table of the Russian characters with their English equivalents. London, 1892. 1 l.
   This follows largely the practice of the British Museum, with minor variations.

298
WIENER, L. The transliteration of Russian. **Library J.**, **23**, 1898. Conference no. 174.

299
ROSENTHAL, H. English spelling of Russian words. **Review of Reviews**, **31**, Jan. 1905:81-83.
   Gives a table of transliteration used by the New York Public Library.

300
GREGORY, J.W. Russian transliteration. **Nature**, **78**, no. 2011, May 14, 1908:42-43.
   On a new system introduced by the Russian Academy, and its advantages and disadvantages compared with the British system (see 295).

301
ŠČERBA, L.V. [Contribution to the problem of transcription.] Izv. Otd. Russk. Jaz. Slov. Imp. Akad. Nauk, **16**, no. 4, 1911: 160-170. (In Russian)

302
FOORD, E. The transliteration of Russian. Nature, 29, no. 2492, Aug. 2, 1917:454-455.
   Tables of the system used by the Academy of Sciences of Petrograd (mainly for the rendering of proper names). At that time the Royal Society was publishing the "International Catalogue of Scientific Literature" and needed a system of transliteration for the names of Russian authors.

303
MONTAGU-NATHAN, M., and S.W. PRING. Russian-English transliteration: a logical method. Musical Times, Nov. 1917: 489-493; Dec. 1917:545-548; Feb. 1918:74-75.

304
CONFERENCE OF UNIVERSITY TEACHERS OF RUSSIAN AND OTHER SLAVONIC LANGUAGES. System of transliteration of Russian. Slavonic Review, 1, 1922/23, preliminary pages.
   The system of transliteration which will be followed by this journal. Table with editorial notes.

305
B., C. Transliteration from Russian into English. Slavonic Review, 13, Jan. 1935:413-419.
   Another new proposal. Each nation should have its own scheme since each attaches different sound-values to many of the Roman characters.

305a
CRANE, E.J. Transliteration of Russian. Industrial and Engineering Chemistry (News ed.), 15, May 20, 1937:230-231.
   Presents the transliteration table used by Chemical Abstracts, which conforms largely to the system used by the Library of Congress.

306
ŠČERBA, L.V. [Transliteration of Russian family names and geographical names into the Roman alphabet.] Izv. Akad. Nauk S.S.S.R. Otd. Lit. Jaz., no. 3, 1940:118-126. (In Russian)

307
HRDLIČKA, A. Russian names. Science, 97, March 12, 1943: 243.
   This short note on the inadequacies of transliteration of Russian names touched off a lively discussion in which participated K. Dunlap (April 30, p.400-401), D.G. Nichols and R.M. Strong (Aug. 6, p. 132-133), P.M. Furfey (Aug. 13, p. 153), Hrdlička (Sept. 3, p. 219), K. Starr-Chester (Oct. 1, p. 302), and V.C. Asmous (Nov. 19, p. 450). The latter pointed out that the Russian name ЖЕЛЕЗНОВ can be found in 7 different places in library catalogs, and the name КУЗНЕЦОВ in 5 places, all of which are under the letter K!

308
BASSET, E. Librarian's guide to title-page Russian and principles of transliteration, with an introduction to Russian law books. New York, Columbia University Libraries Press, 1944. 47 l.
 A thorough treatment of the problem and a discussion of the various transliteration systems in use. There is a comprehensive annotated bibliography.

309
HARRINGTON, J.P. New method of transliterating Russian. J. Washington Academy of Sciences, 34, April 1944:108-110.

310
KOSOLAPOFF, G.M. Transliteration of Russian words. Science, June 16, 1944:491-492; Feb. 16, 1945:175.
 Advocates the use of the Chemical Abstracts system, to avoid ambiguities. Rejoinder by J.B. Hickman, May 14, 1945: 460.

311
PALMER, F.M. Value of Russian to reference librarians. College and Research Libraries, 6, June 1945:195-198.
 On the difficulties of transliteration by various national schemes, all of which find their way into libraries. Also on the translation of Russian periodical titles without indication of source language which leads to confusion.

312
THOMSON, H. N. Chart of transliteration and Latin alphabet systems for the Russian language. Bull. AATSEEL, 4, no. 1, 1946:37-38.
 A synoptic table of 13 systems of transliteration found in the published literature.

313
KARUM, L.S. [On the Romanization of Russian family names and geographical names.] Voprosy Jazykoznanija, 1953:102-105. (In Russian)

314
MORISON, W.A. How to type Russian on an English machine. Slavonic and East European Review, 32, 1953-54:509-511.
 All Cyrillic letters (except Л) can be simulated on a regular Roman letter typewriter by using combinations of letters, numerals and signs.

315
GILJAREVSKIJ, R.S. [Cataloging of Soviet works translated into foreign languages; method of transliteration.] Sovetskaja Bibliografija, 1955:31. (In Russian)
 Transliteration for Russian, virtually identical with the one later adopted by ISO (see 222), but Ukrainian and White-Russian are not considered.

316
RICHTER, Erich. Vergleichende Transkriptionstabelle als

Hilfsmittel zum Auffinden russischer Schriften in den grossen internationalen Allgemeinbibliographien; mit Erläuterungen. [Comparative transcription table as a finding aid for Russian works in the great international general bibliographies; with explanations.] Göttingen, 1955. 7, ii l.

    The transliteration systems used by the <u>Deutscher Gesamtkatalog</u> (and the then recently renewed <u>Berliner Titeldrucke</u>), the <u>Bibliographie nationale</u> (France), the printed catalogs of the British Museum, the Library of Congress and the Kungliga biblioteket (Stockholm), all of which use different systems. Bibliographers and librarians must make themselves familiar with them in order to find entries for Russian works.

317
RAZRAN, G. Transliteration of Russian. <u>Science</u>, <u>129</u>, no. 3356, April 24, 1959:1111-1113.
    Proposes a kind of hybrid system, combining transliteration and transcription.

318
Russian-English transliteration. <u>Science</u>, <u>130</u>, no. 3374, Aug. 28, 1959:482-488.
    Under this heading, four replies to Razran's proposal (see 317) by E.P. Hamp, A.C. Fabergé, M.B. and I.D. London and D.T. Ray are published, all of which reject his ideas for various reasons. Razran then replies. Later, he and G. Susich published a further rejoinder (<u>Science</u>, <u>131</u>, no. 3397, Feb. 5, 1960:324.).

319
REFORMATSKIJ, A.A. [Transliteration of Russian texts in Roman characters.] <u>Voprosy Jazykoznanija</u>, <u>9</u>, 1960:96-103. (In Russian)

320
NEISWENDER, R. Russian transliteration - sound and sense. <u>Special Libraries</u>, <u>53</u>, 1962:37-41.
    On the confusion created by the use of different schemes. Contains a bibliography. There is a critical reply by G. Gerych, with Neiswender's rejoinder, p. 555-557.

321
BATTELLE MEMORIAL INSTITUTE. Directory of selected scientific institutions in the USSR. Columbus, Ohio, 1963.
    There is a "Comparative table of major transliteration systems" on p. 4, which displays the schemes used by the Library of Congress, the British Standards Institute, the Board on Geographic Names, ISO, the New York Public Library, <u>Slavonic Review</u> and <u>Mathematical Reviews</u>.

322
ORNE, J. Transliteration of modern Russian. <u>Library J.</u>, <u>88</u>, Nov. 1, 1963:4157-4160.

323
ORNE, J. Transliteration of modern Russian. <u>Library Resources and Technical Services</u>, <u>8</u>, Winter 1964:51-52.
    This article and item 322 consider the conversion of one written language into another, with particular reference to Russian, and the principles of a forthcoming American Standard on transliteration of Cyrillic characters.

324
JAKOBSON, R.O. [On the Romanization of international telegrams in Russian.] <u>Voprosy Jazykoznanija</u>, <u>14</u>, no. 1, 1965: 111-113. (In Russian)
    A new transliteration system, using several digraphs.

325
FRANKLIN, D. Reversible punctuation Russian transliteration. <u>American Documentation</u>, <u>17</u>, July 1966:142-145.
    A new transliteration scheme, making extensive use of punctuation marks to assure complete reversibility. There are also tables of transliteration for Armenian, Georgian, Hebrew and Yiddish, using the same system. The system has probably not been used by anyone but the author. There is an extensive bibliography.

326
CROME, H. Die Uebertragung russischer Personennamen ins Englische. [The transliteration of Russian personal names into English.] <u>Fremdsprachen</u>, 1967:104-106.

327
SHAW, J.T. Transliteration of modern Russian for English-language publications. Madison, University of Wisconsin Press, 1967. 15 p.
    Presents four systems for different uses: System I is for popular use; System II is the Library of Congress scheme without diacritical marks, System III is the ISO system, both of which are stated to be "for citations of bibliographical material"; and System IV is again the LC system, but with diacritical marks, to be used "for separate bibliographical publications". A "Mixture of systems" is also discussed, and there is a comparative table of Russian names and dates.

328
USPENSKIJ, V.A. [On the problem of transliteration of Russian texts in Roman characters.] <u>Naučno-tehničeskaja Informacija</u>, ser. 2, no. 7, 1967:12-20. (In Russian)
    The function of translation, transcription and transliteration are defined. Seven basic requirements for transliteration from Russian into Roman characters are listed.

329
UNITED STATES. CENTRAL INTELLIGENCE AGENCY. Russian personal names. Washington, D.C., 1968. viii, 161 p.
    A guide for the searching and recording of Soviet personal names by non-specialists. There are 11 tables of trans-

literation, using the system of the Board on Geographic names: Russian-English, Russian-Other Slavic languages, Russian-Germanic languages, Russian-Baltic languages, Russian-Finno-Ugric languages, Russian-English-French, Russian-English-Spanish, Russian-Vietnamese-French-English, Russian-Albanian-Greek-Italian-Rumanian-Turkish-English, Non-Slavic Cyrillic alphabet languages-English, and Armenian to English and Russian. Explanations on the structure of Russian personal names and titles are also given, and the work concludes with an alphabetic list of Russian names and their diminutives. This seems to be the most comprehensive compilation of its kind. It is unclassified and therefore available in libraries.

330
CHAREN, T. MEDLARS indexing manual. Bethesda, Md., National Library of Medicine, 1972. 520 p.
   Section 10. Titles: foreign titles (p. 119-131) deals with transliteration of titles in Greek, Bulgarian, Russian and Ukrainian (other languages are not to be transliterated in the MEDLARS system). There is a transliteration table for Cyrillic characters, taken from the Russian-English Medical Dictionary by S. Jablonski, not using any diacritical marks, but otherwise similar to LC.

                    Russian-Spanish
331
FERNÁNDEZ-GALIANO, M. Sobre la transliteración del griego y el ruso. [On the transliteration of Greek and Russian.] Filología Moderna, 31-32, 1968:277-292.

                    Russian-German
332
JAHR, W. Transkription russischer Eigennamen. [Transcription of Russian proper names.] Zentralbl. Bibliothekswesen, 25, 1908:132-133.

334
Regeln zur Transkription von russischen Eigen- und Familiennamen, erdkundlichen Namen, Titeln, u.a. im deutschen Schrifttum. [Rules for the transcription of Russian proper names and surnames, geographical names, titles, etc. in the German literature.] Leipzig, SWA-Verlag, 1947. 3 p.

335
DIEHL, E. Die Umschrift russischer Wörter mit deutschen Buchstaben. [The Romanization of Russian words with German letters.] Russischunterricht, 1, 1948:50-57.

336
OLESCH, R. Zum Transkriptionsproblem des Russischen. [On the transcription problem of Russian.] Russischunterricht, 1, 1948:99-103.

337
STEINITZ, W. Wie sollen wir russische Namen schreiben?
[How should we write Russian names?] Die neue Gesellschaft,
2, Nr. 4, 1948:66-71; 4, Nr. 3, 1950:233.

338
HERMENAU, O. Ein entscheidender Schritt zur Vereinheitlichung der deutschen Schreibung russischer Wörter. [A decisive step towards unification of the German spelling of Russian words.] Russischunterricht, 2, 1949:98.

339
Einheitliche Schreibung russischer Wörter. [Uniform spelling of Russian words.] Bibliothekar, 4, Nr. 2, 1950:111-112.

340
HAYKIN, D.J. Russian transliteration in Germany. Library of Congress Information Bulletin, 10, May 28, 1951:12-13.
    A short survey of present trends in German cataloging.

341
KRAL, W. Eine neue Transkription russischer Titel? [A new transcription of Russian entries?] Zentralbl. Bibliothekswesen, 65, Nr. 1, 1951:61-65.
    Despite several recent attempts to "simplify" the transliteration of Russian, libraries in the Russian zone of Germany will be best advised to keep to the proven scheme of the "Prussian instructions" (see 87).

342
KRAL, W. Zur Transkription des russischen Alphabets im "Duden", Ausgabe 1951. [On the transcription of the Russian alphabet in the 1951 edition of Duden.] Zentralbl. Bibliothekswesen, 66, Nr. 1, 1952:47-50.
    Discusses the system used by the (East-German) edition of the standard dictionary Duden which follows a scheme proposed by W. Steinitz (see also 337). Libraries in Germany will still use the scheme in "Prussian instructions (see 87).

343
DICK, G., and F. KRETSCHMAR. Zur Transkription des russischen Alphabets. [On the transcription of the Russian alphabet.] Russischunterricht, 7, 1954:15ff.

344
MÜHLPFORDT, G. Transkriptionsprobleme. [Problems of transcription.] Leipzig, Rütten & Loening, 1957. 175 p.
    A comprehensive treatise on the problems posed by the transcription of Russian names in the German literature. Particular attention is paid to re-transliteration of Russian and non-Russian names, for which purpose the author and a collaborator, K. Diesing, compiled tables of names and their proper re-transliteration.

345
ŠČERBINA, N. Zur Frage der "richtigen" Namensschreibung bei

Uebersetzungen. [On the question of the "correct" spelling of names in translations.] <u>Dokumentation</u>, <u>6</u>, 1959:50-52.
   On the spelling of Russian personal names in German translation.

346
SCHADE, W. Transkriptionsprobleme. [Problems of transcription.] <u>Fremdsprachen</u>, 1960:176-180.

347
BRUHN, P. Zum Problem der Durchsetzung einer einheitlichen, volkstümlichen deutschen Umschrift russischer Namen. [On the problem of the enforcement of a uniform, popular German Romanization of Russian names.] <u>Osteuropa</u>, <u>11</u>, 1961:413-414.

348
RECK, H.F. Zum Problem der Umschreibung russischer Namen. [On the problem of Romanization of Russian names.] <u>Osteuropa</u>, <u>11</u>, 1961:746-747.

349
SCHMID, A. and FRI[TSCHY, G.J.M.] Zur Transkription der russischen Schrift. [On the transcription of the Russian script.] <u>Lebende Sprachen</u>, <u>6</u>, 1961:141-142.

350
DUDEN. Rechtschreibung der deutschen Sprache und der Fremdwörter. [Orthography of the German language and foreign words.] 15., erw. Aufl. Mannheim, Bibliographisches Institut, 1962. (Der Grosse Duden, Bd. 1)
   Transkription und Transliteration aus dem Russischen. [Transcription and transliteration from the Russian.] p. 795-797. This is the West-German edition of the standard German dictionary, whose transliteration table is now considerably different from the one used in the East-German edition (see 342).

351
WINKLER, J. Die Transliteration von Namen, Bezeichnungen und Orten aus der russischen Sprache. [The transliteration of names, designations and places from the Russian.] <u>Dokumentation</u>, <u>11</u>, 1964:10-13.
   Transcription is rejected for documentation purposes, because only transliteration makes it possible to identify uniquely names of authors, agencies, institutions, place names, etc. But the original form of non-Russian names should be restored as far as possible.

352
BAYERL, B., and H. CROME. Zur Transkription aus dem Russischen. [On transcription from Russian.] <u>Fremdsprachen</u>, 1966:96-99.

353
RAAB, H. Zur Frage der Transliteration russischer Wörter im Deutschen. [On the question of transliteration of Russian words in German.] <u>Wiss. Z. Univ. Rostock, Ges. Sprachwiss.</u>, <u>15</u>, 1966:651-658.

354
ZIKMUND, H. Die deutsche Umschrift der russischen Zisch-
lautbuchstaben. [The German Romanization of Russian letters for sibilants.] <u>Wiss. Z. Humboldt-Univ. Berlin, Ges.
sprachwiss. R.</u>, <u>16</u>, 1967:687-690.
   On the transliteration of Ч, Ш, Щ.

355
BRUHN, P. Russisch für Bibliothekare; Leitfaden für die Be-
arbeitung von russischem Schrifttum in wissenschaftlichen
Bibliotheken. [Russian for librarians; guide for the treatment of Russian literature in research libraries.] Wiesbaden, Harrassowitz, 1968. 75 p.
   A practical guide for the cataloging of Russian works
   for German librarians. Transliteration tables show
   the German system (Prussian instructions), the French and
   Anglo-American systems. Rules for the re-transliteration of German, English and French personal names are given. A comparative table shows the differences in transliteration according to the East- and West-German editions
   of <u>Duden</u>. Annotated bibliography of 53 works in German
   and Russian.

356
HÄUSLER, F. Zur Frage einer phonetischen Transkription des
Russischen. [On the question of a phonetic transcription
of Russian.] <u>Fremdsprachenunterricht</u>, <u>12</u>, 1968:216-220.

356a
HÄUSLER, F. Die Lautschrift der API und die phonetische
Transkription des Russischen. [The phonetic alphabet of API
and the phonetic transcription of Russian.] <u>Fremdsprachen</u>,
1968:12-22.

357
LAUCH, A. Russisch-deutsche Transkription im 18. Jahrhundert.
[Russian-German transcription in the 18th century.] <u>In</u> <u>Stud.
Gesch. russ. Lit.</u> [C], 1968. Vol. 3, p.243-254, 570-574.

358
RAAB, H. Die Transliteration als Teilproblem der sprachli-
chen Kommunikation. <u>Fremdsprachen</u>, 1968:111-115.
   On "popular" vs. "scientific" transliteration. Some short-
   comings of the (East-German) <u>Duden</u> system are pointed out.

359
RAAB, H. Zu einigen theoretischen Aspekten der deutschen Umschrift russischer Wörter. [On some theoretical aspects of
the German Romanization of Russian.] <u>In</u> <u>Slavisch-deutsche
Wechselbeziehungen</u> [C], 1969. p. 148-154.

                    Russian-Dutch
360
WIJK, N. van De translitteratie van Russische eigennamen.
[The transliteration of Russian personal names.] 2e verm.
dr. s'Gravenhage, Uitgeversfonds der Biblioteekvereeniging-
en, 1939. 16 p. (Leeszaalwerk no. 5)

361
THYS, E. De transkriptie van de Russische eigennamen. [The transcription of Russian personal names.] Biblioteeksgids, 25, May-June 1949:38-41.
  Compares the schemes used in different countries and those proposed by Dutch philologists and van Wijk (see 360).

Russian-Bulgarian

362
ANDREJČIN, L. [Transcription and pronunciation of some Russian words with ě.] Bălgarski Ezik, 17, 1967:488-489. (In Bulgarian)

Russian-Slovakian

363
JONA, E. Ako prepisovat' ruské mená v slovenčine. [Transcription of Russian names into Slovakian.] Slovenska Reč, 15, 1949-50:141-148.

Russian-Polish

364
MIROWICZ, A., and JAKUBOWSKI, W. Jeszcze w sprawie transkrypcji rosyjskiej. [Again on the problem of transcription of Russian.] Język Polski, 43, 1963:277-279.
  Discusses various schemes of transliteration of Russian names into Polish.

Russian-Finnish

365
VAHROS, I., and M. KAHLA. Venäläisten sanojen translitteroinnista. [On the transliteration of Russian words.] Neuvostoliittoinstituutia Vuosikirja, 11/14, 1959-1963:137-145.

***

See also 84, 87, 90, 213, 221, 222, 224, 226, 234-236, 253, 259, 260. Place names 711, 716-720.

Ukrainian

Romanization

See 87, 90, 222, 224, 226, 234-236, 253, 259, 261, 711.

Ukrainian-Bulgarian

366
ANDREJČIN, L. [Pronunciation and transcription of Ukrainian names.] Bălgarski Ezik, 19, 1969:171-175 (In Bulgarian)

Ukrainian-Arabic

367
STANKIEVICH, J. The importance of the Arabic alphabet in the monuments of the White Ruthenian language. Washington, D.C., 1953. 33 l.

White-Russian

White=Russian-Hungarian

368
DESZÖ, L. A fehérorosz és makedón címek átírásáról. [Transliteration of White-Russian and Macedonian titles.] Magyar Könyvszemle, 77, Oct. 1961:520-521.

White=Russian-Bulgarian

369
ANDREJČIN, L. [Pronunciation and transcription of White-Russian names.] Bǎlgarski Ezik, 20, 1970:38-41. (In Bulgarian)

***

See also 90, 222, 224, 226, 234-236, 253, 257, 259, 261.

Cyrillization

Transcription of non-Cyrillic scripts in general into Cyrillic script.

370
JUŠMANOV, N.V. [Key to Roman script on globes.] Moskva, Akademija Nauk SSSR, 1941. (In Russian)

371
AMBURGER, E. Die Behandlung ausländischer Vornamen im Russischen in neuerer Zeit. [The treatment of foreign forenames in Russian in recent times.] Abhandl. Akad. Wiss. Lit. Mainz, Geistes- Sozialwiss. Kl., 1953:299-354.

372
ŠNITKE, G.V. [On the transliteration of proper names.] Voprosy Jazykoznanija, 1954:126-129. (In Russian)

373
SUPERANSKAJA, A.V. [On some questions of practical transcription.] Voprosy Jazykoznanija, 1955:99-104. (In Russian)

374
BERKOV, V.P. [Letter to the editor.] Voprosy Jazykoznanija, 1958:152. (In Russian)
  On mistakes made in the transcription of foreign names. Urges standardization of transcription rules from foreign languages and scripts into Cyrillic.

375
KIPARSKY, V. Foreign h in Russian. Slavonic and East European Review, 38, 1960:82-94.
  Until about 1910, h was mostly transliterated by г. After 1917, it is more often transliterated by х, probably due to the influence of Finnish, in which h is aspirated.

376
REFORMATSKIJ, A.A. [Practical transcription of proper names in foreign languages.] Izv. Akad. Nauk SSSR, Otd. Lit. Jaz., 19, 1960:529-534. (In Russian)

377
UBRIATOVA, YE.I. [Problems of script and orthography in the languages of the peoples of the USSR who use alphabets based on the Russian.] In Voprosy terminologii [C] 1961. p. 92-99. (In Russian)
   The alphabets of many peoples in the USSR were originally based on the Roman. In the 1930'ies there was a move towards Cyrillization and today most non-Slavic languages in the Soviet Union are written in Cyrillic. But while Roman script was fairly uniform, the Cyrillic characters and additional letters are not. Unification is desirable because now the literature of these peoples can be read only in the area where it is written.

378
LEONT'EV, A.A. [On the spelling of foreign names.] Kultury Reči, 4, 1963:154-156. (In Russian)
   On the difficulties in transliteration and transcription of names in foreign languages, especially English.

379
GILJAREVSKIJ, R.S., and V.S. GRIVNIN. [Manual for the identification of the languages of the world, on the basis of written specimens.] 3rd ed. Moskva, "Nauka", 1964. 375 p. (In Russian)
   Mainly written as an aid in bibliographical work. The problem of transliteration and transcription is also dealt with, where Western languages in Roman script are concerned. See also the first author's manual on transcription of names (388).

380
KALAKUCKAJA, L.P. [The orthographic transliteration of long consonants in proper names as printed in foreign languages.] In Orfografija sobstvennih imen [C], 1964. p. 90-103. (In Russian.)
   On the rendering of double consonants in Russian which leads to difficulties and variations of spelling.

381
KOLJADA, G.I. [Writing double consonants in foreign words.] Nauč. Trudy Taškent. Gos. Univ., Filol. Nauki, 1964:3-14. (In Russian)

382
MAKSIMOVA, L.K. [Some difficult cases of e, je, ju and ja in the spelling of foreign proper names.] In Orfografija sobstvennih imen [C], 1964. p. 81-89. (In Russian)

383
Orfografija sobstvennih imen. [Orthography of proper names.] Edited by A.A. Reformatskij. Moskva, "Nauka", 1964. 145 p. (In Russian)

A collection of articles on problems of orthography of names, both Russian and foreign. See also 380, 382, 384, 734, 735.

384
STAL'TMAN, V.E. [Transcription of proper names as one word, several words or hyphenated?] In Orfografija sobstvennih imen [C], 1964. p. 44-80. (In Russian)

385
TOLSTOJ, I.I. [Notes on Slavic proper names and their transcription.] In Toponomastika i transkripcija [C], 1964. (In Russian)

386
STAROSTIN, B.A. [Transcription of proper names; practical manual.] Edited by R.S. Giljarevskij. 2nd ed. Moskva, "Kniga", 1965. 90 p. (In Russian)
On the rendering of names in 82 national languages spoken and written in the Soviet Union, using the Cyrillic or the Roman alphabets.

387
Toponomastika i transkripcija. [The study of place names and transcription.] Edited by S.G. Barhudarov et al. Moskva, "Nauka", 1964. 199 p. (In Russian)
A collection of articles on problems in the transcription of place names and proper names.

388
GILJAREVSKIJ, R.S. and B.A. STAROSTIN. [Foreign names and designations in Russian texts; reference book.] Moskva, Izd. Meždunarodnye Otnošenja, 1969. 216 p. (In Russian)
A bibliographical manual, explaining the principles of pronunciation of foreign names, the principles of their phonetic transcription into Russian Cyrillic, and listing the most commonly occurring forenames of the following languages: Bulgarian, Czech, Danish, Dutch, English, Finnish, French, German, Hungarian, Italian, Norwegian, Polish, Portuguese, Romanian, Serbo-Croatian, Slovakian, Spanish, Swedish. The largest section is devoted to English which poses the most difficult problems of transcription because of its largely non-phonetic spelling.

***

See also 29, 418 and entries under Cyrillization in the Subject index.

III. ORIENTAL LANGUAGES

Transcription into Greek

390
ZETTERSTÉEN, K.V. Några orientaliska ord i grekisk transskription. [Some oriental words in Greek transcription.] Monde Oriental, 6, 1912:193-200.

See also 419.

Romanization

391
JONES, Sir W. A dissertation on the orthography of Asiatick words in Roman letters. Asiatick Researches, 1, 1788:1-56.
  The opening article of the new journal devoted to research on Asia dealt with the necessity of finding a generally applicable transliteration methods for the main languages of Asia, primarily Arabic, Persian and the Indic vernaculars. Almost all subsequent writers on the subject during the 19th century based their work on Jones' proposals. The article was later reprinted in The works of Sir William Jones. London, 1807. Vol. 3, p. 253-318.

392
VOLNEY, C.-F. Simplification des langues orientales, ou méthode nouvelle et facile d'apprendre les langues arabe, persane et turque avec des caractères européens. [Simplification of oriental languages, or new and easy method to render the Arabic, Persian and Turkish languages with European characters.] Paris, Imprimerie de la république, III [i.e. 1794]. 135 p.
  Volney was one of the last "encyclopédistes", an orientalist who had travelled widely through Asia and the Near East. He proposed a systematic alphabet for transcription, and his system was actually used for the rendering of place names on the map of Egypt which was compiled in 1803 as part of Description de l'Egypte.

393
LANGLÈS, L.M. Note du cen Langlès sur la manière d'orthographier les mots orientaux. [Notes by citizen Langlès on the manner of spelling of Oriental words.] Notices et extraits des manuscrits de la Bibliothèque nationale, 5, an VII [i.e. 1798-99]:4-8.
  A critique of Volney's scheme.

394
VOLNEY, C.-F. L'Alfabet européen appliquée aux langues asiatiques; ouvrage élémentaire utile à tout voyageur en Asie. [The European alphabet applied to Asian languages; elementary treatise, useful for any traveller in Asia.] Paris, Firmin-Didot, 1819. xviii, 223 p.
  An enlarged and revised edition of 392.

395
MARSDEN, W. Bibliotheca Marsdeniana philologica et orientalis. A catalogue of books and manuscripts collected with a view to the general comparison of language, and to the study of Oriental literature. London, Cox, 1827. 308 p.

396
MARSDEN, W. On a conventional Roman alphabet, applicable to Oriental languages. In his Miscellaneous works. London, Parbury, Allen & Co., 1834. Vol. 2.

397
TREVELYAN, Sir C.E. The application of the Roman alphabet to all Oriental languages; contained in a series of papers written by Messrs. Trevelyan, J. Prinsep, and Tytler, Rev. A. Duff, and Mr. H.T. Prinsep, and published in various Calcutta periodicals in the year 1834. Serampore, 1834. 162 p.

398
TREVELYAN, Sir C.E. Circular letter addressed by the originators of the general application of the Roman letters to the languages of the East. Calcutta, 1834.

399
TREVELYAN, Sir C.E. The Romanizing system. Calcutta, 1836.

400
TREVELYAN, Sir C.E. Papers originally published at Calcutta in 1834 and 1836 on the application of the Roman letters to the languages of Asia. London, 1854.

401
Report of the Transliteration Committee [of the Royal Asiatic Society of Great Britain and Ireland]. J. Roy. Asiat. Soc., 1894. 13 p.
   Transliteration schemes for Sanskrit, Pali and Arabic, and additional tables for some other languages.

402
BURGESS, J. The transliteration of Oriental alphabets. In Actes du dixième Congrès International des Orientalistes, 1894. Leide, 1895.   p. 27-42 of Deuxième partie.

403
Tenth International Congress of Orientalists, held at Geneva. Report of the Transliteration Committee. (Translation.) J. Roy. Asiat. Soc., 1895:879-892.
   The transliteration systems proposed by the Committee for Sanskrit, Prakrit, Arabic, followed by an account of the Committee's work by G.T. Plunkett. This English version was published before the official transcript of the Congress proceedings were published in French (see below 404).

404
Rapport de la Commission de transcription. In Actes du dixième Congrès International des Orientalistes, 1894. Session de Genève. Leide, 1896. 15 p. at end of Troisième partie.

405
Transliteration. <u>J. Roy. Asiat. Soc.</u>, 1896. p. 1-12 at end of volume after p. 835.
   The report of a committee appointed by the Society on the motion of Sir M. Monier-Williams. The transliteration schemes cover Sanskrit and other Indic languages written in the Devanagari script, Arabic and Hebrew. The tables were reprinted in the April and October issues of the <u>Journal</u> for 1913 and subsequent years.

406
PEISER, F.E. Zur Transcriptionsfrage. [On the question of transcription.] <u>Orientalistische Litteraturzeitung</u>, 1903: 360.

407
HÜSING, G. Zur Transskriptionsfrage. <u>Orientalistische Litteraturzeitung</u>, 1904:46.

408
BROWN, R.G. The use of the Roman character for Oriental languages. <u>J. Roy. Asiat. Soc.</u>, 1912:647-663.
   Deals mostly with Indic languages, but discusses also other Asian vernaculars.

409
RONDOT, P. La latinisation des alphabets orientaux. [The Romanization of Oriental alphabets.] <u>Renseignements Coloniaux</u>, 1938:76-78.

410
SCHUBERT, J. Transkription orientalischer und ostasiatischer Schriften. [Transcription of Oriental and East Asian scripts.] <u>Dokumentation und Arbeitstechnik</u>, 1940:3-4.

411
RANGANATHAN, S.R. Asian names. <u>Abgila</u>, <u>3</u>, no. 2, June 1953:45-54.
   The scope of the Unesco project on rendering of Asian names is explained. Various Asian cataloging practices are outlined and compared with European practices.

412
SPALDING, C.S. Transliteration of vernacular alphabets; cooperative cataloging of vernacular materials; and cataloging treatment of pamphlet materials. <u>In Conference on American Library Resources in Southern Asia</u>, Washington, D.C., 1957. 27 p. (Working paper no. 8)
   Deals with the transcription of Arabic and the scripts of South-East Asian languages.

413
ELAHI, F., et al. Cataloguing of Oriental names. <u>Pakistan Library Association Quarterly Journal</u>, <u>2</u>, July 1961:5-16.

414
SPALDING, C.S. International standards in Orientalist cat-

aloging. <u>Library of Congress Inform. Bull.</u>, <u>30</u>, no. 6, Feb. 11, 1972:A 29.
   The author chaired a seminar on the subject at the 28th International Congress of Orientalists, Canberra, 1971. The cataloging, transliteration and transcription of Arabic, Chinese and Indonesian names were discussed.

414a
ČESKOSLOVENSKE TISKOVÉ KANCELÁŘE. DOKUMENTAČNÍ ODDĚLENÍ ZAHRANIČNI REDAKCE. Jak přepisovat z orientálnich jazyků. [How to transcribe from Oriental languages.] Praha [n.d.]

415
KEMPF, Z. Orientalna transkrypcja czy transliteracja? [An Oriental transcription or a transliteration?] <u>Przegład Orientalistyczny</u>, <u>31</u>, 1939:311-320.

416
ZAJACZKOWSKI, W. O poprawna pisownie imion i nazw orientalnych. [On an improved spelling of Oriental names and designations.] <u>Przegład Orientalistyczny</u>, 1954:296-297.

Cyrillization

417
[Materials on the unification of bibliographical transcription of the scripts of Oriental peoples.] <u>Vostočnij Sbornik</u>, 1926:193-200. (In Russian)

418
SERDJUČENKO, G.P. [On Russian transcriptions of Oriental languages.] <u>Problemy Vostokovedenija</u>, no. 3, 1960:91-107.
   How to render single words or short phrases in Oriental languages in Russian texts. Two systems are needed: one for popular use, for the press and for cartography; another, for the use of orientalists, dictionaries, etc. Standardization is badly needed, but there is as yet no basis for it in the Cyrillic alphabet. Examples are drawn from Arabic, Persian, Turkish, Hindi, Pushto, Korean, Mongolian, Japanese and Chinese. (In Russian)

IV. HAMITO-SEMITIC LANGUAGES

Transcription into Greek

419
PREISIGKE, F. Namenbuch, enthaltend alle griechischen, lateinischen, ägyptischen, hebräischen, arabischen und sonstigen semitischen und nicht-semitischen Menschennamen, soweit sie in griechischen Urkunden ... Aegyptens sich vorfinden. [Name-book, containing all Greek, Latin, Egyptian, Hebrew, Arabic and other Semitic and non-Semitic names of persons, inasmuch as they appear in Greek documents ... of Egypt.] Heidelberg, 1922.

The work consists almost entirely of lists of names in the languages enumerated and their transcription into Greek as found on papyri, stone monuments and clay tablets. In his preface, the author states: "The names have been transmitted in various spellings, according to the variant pronunciations and spellings of the time (variant forms)". The work has been reprinted (Amsterdam, Hakkert, 1967).

Romanization

420
KOOPMANS, J. Ein Vorschlag zur Transliteration (semitischer) Sprachen. [A proposal for the transliteration of (Semitic) languages.] Bibliotheca Orientalis, 12, 1955:46-48.
   On a new transliteration scheme for Hebrew and Arabic, not using any diacritical marks in order to save on printing costs of orientalistic literature.

421
GOLDMAN, E.A., H.D.U. SMITH, and R.D. TANENBAUM. A "computer-compatible" Semitic alphabet. Hebrew Union College Annual, 42, 1971:251-278.
   A scheme for unambiguous transliteration of both consonants and vowel signs (points) in Hebrew, Yiddish, Syriac and Ugaritic for the use of computers. The Roman letters and signs and symbols available on a regular printchain are used. The resulting transliteration from Hebrew etc. is not intelligible to a reader familiar with the original script, but it is uniquely reversible, so that a conversion program (not considered by the authors in this context) could reproduce the original text from computer printout.

Cyrillization

422
ZAVADOVSKIJ, YU. N. [On a systematic transcription and transliteration for Hamito-Semitic languages.] Semitske Jazyki, 1963:171-175. (In Russian)
   Transcription schemes for Assyrian, Syriac, Arabic, Amharic, Hebrew, Coptic, Ugaritic, Berber, Haussa.

***

See also 10, 15.

Hebrew

Romanization

423
BACON, R. The Opus Majus ... edited, with introd. and analytical table, by J.H. Bridges. Oxford, 1897-1900. 3 v.
   "Linguarum cognitio", vol. i, p. 74-77, and in Supplementary vol., p. 89-94. Transliteration table for Hebrew on p. 74. The frontispiece is a facsimile of MS

Vatican 4086, f. 15b, 16a, showing the transliteration tables for Hebrew and Greek. One of the earliest attempts at a systematic transliteration of Hebrew into Roman script.

423a
BRUTIS, PETRUS DE Victoria contra Iudaeos. [Victory against the Jews.] Vicenza, Simon Bevilaqua, 1489. [130] l. (Ges. Kat. Wiegendr., Bd. 5, no. 5659)
   This incunabulum is probably the first printed book to contain Romanized passages of Hebrew. In order to reinforce his arguments against the Jews, the author cites passages from the Bible and transliterates the Hebrew phonetically, as he pronounced it in his northern Italian dialect. The book contains also a passage in transliterated Turkish (see 512).

424
GESSNER, C. Mithridates. De differentiis linguarum, tum veterum tum quae hodie apud diversas nationes in toto orbē terrarum in usu sunt Conradi Gesneri observationes. [Mithridates. Observations on the differences of languages, ancient as well as those which today are in use with diverse nations all over the world, by Conrad Gessner.] Tiguri, Excudebat Froschoverus, 1555. [2], 78 l.
   In this work, the famous Renaissance polyhistor tried his hand at comparative linguistics. He considers Hebrew to be "the first and oldest language" from which all others are derived by successive "corruption". In a fold-out table at the end of the volume the Lord's Prayer is printed in 22 languages; the Hebrew version is printed in Hebrew square letters and in a phonetic transliteration (following the Sephardic pronunciation) in black letter.

425
BARGÈS, J.J.L. Le Livre de Ruth, expliqué par deux traductions françaises, l'une littérale ... accompagnée de la transcription des mots hébreux ... [The Book of Ruth, explained by two French translations, one literal ... accompanied by the transcription of the Hebrew words ...] Paris, Leroux & Jouby, 1854.
   This is one of the first transliteration systems for Hebrew on a scientific basis, intended for the use of orientalists. Although quite clumsy, it was widely used in France during the 19th century for philological purposes.

426
THE JEWISH ENCYCLOPEDIA. New York, Funk & Wagnall, 1901-05.
   There is an article on Transliteration [of Hebrew] in vol. 12, p. 229-231 which gives an historical account of transliteration from and into Hebrew, with many examples from Greek, Latin and Arabic. The system of transliteration used by the Encyclopedia itself is explained in vol. 1, p. xxv.

427
JÜDISCHES LEXIKON. [Jewish Lexicon.] Berlin, Jüdischer Verlag, 1927-34.
"Transkription hebräischer Wörter" [Transcription of Hebrew words] in vol. 1, p. xiv-xv. The system is phonetic, based on German spelling (but following the Sephardic pronunciation).

428
PALESTINE. GOVERNMENT. Transliteration from Arabic and Hebrew into English, from Arabic into Hebrew, and from Hebrew into Arabic, with transliterated lists of personal and geographic names for use in Palestine. Jerusalem, Goldberg's Press, 1931. 85 p.
Issued by the Palestine Government as its official code of transliteration.

429
BRUX, A.A. Simplified system of Hebrew-English and Aramaic-English transliteration. Amer. J. Semit. Lang., 58, Jan. 1941:57-69.
Argues for the use of transliteration and emphasizes the importance of the "Schriftbild" as against the "Lautbild" of the Semitic languages.

430
THE UNIVERSAL JEWISH ENCYCLOPEDIA. New York, 1939-43.
Has a table of Hebrew transliteration in vol. 1, p. 202, which differs somewhat from the one used by 426.

431
JABOTINSKY, Z. Hebrew without tears. Taryag millim. 613 (Hebrew) words. Introduction into spoken Hebrew (in Latin characters). London, Jewish Publ., 1950. 104 p.
An attempt to introduce Western adults to the most commonly used Hebrew words, transliterated by the author's own system which makes ample use of diacritical marks. Contrary to popular myth, this was not an attempt to Latinize Hebrew, but only to popularize its use. In the foreword Jabotinsky says: "The fact that Latin transcription only is used in the booklet has nothing to do with the question whether Latin characters should or should not be adopted generally for printing Hebrew books or newspapers."

432
ACADEMY OF THE HEBREW LANGUAGE. [Rules for the transliteration of Hebrew script into Roman script.] Jerusalem, 1957. (In Hebrew)
This is the official scheme used by the Israeli government. It was published in a "broad" and a "scholarly" version; the latter formed the basis for the subsequent ISO scheme (see 434). The discussions of the Academy prior to publication of the scheme are published in Zikhronot ha-aqademya, 1-2, 1953-54:59-85; 3-4, 1957:30-33, 35-40, 46-51, 54-56.

433
POULAIN, J. transliteration of Hebrew characters. Unesco Bull. Libr., 15, Nov.-Dec. 1961:329-330, 333.
  Rejects the ISO scheme (then in draft form) and proposes a pure transliteration of consonants only, independent of pronunciation, as the only useful system for bibliographical purposes. There is an editorial reply in 16, July 1962:212-213 which is based on the arguments of an ISO expert.   For Poulain's rejoinder see 436.

434
INTERNATIONAL ORGANIZATION FOR STANDARDIZATION. Transliteration of Hebrew. 1st ed. Geneva, 1962. 7 p. (ISO/R259)
  This follows almost exactly the Academy of the Hebrew Language scheme (except for the transliteration of some vowels).

435
EDELMANN, R. The treatment of names in Hebrew characters and title entry for Hebrew books. In: International conference on cataloguing principles. Paris, 1961. London, IFLA, 1963. p. 277-279.

436
POULAIN, J. Transliteration of Hebrew characters. Unesco Bull.Libr., 17, Jan.-Feb. 1963:43-44.
  Rejects the opinions of the ISO expert (see 433) and insists on transliteration with complete reversibility and some indication of pronunciation if possible. The Israeli system is also rejected as unsuitable for bibliographical purposes.

437
ASSOCIATION FRANÇAISE DE NORMALISATION. Translittération de l'hebreu en caractères latins. [Transliteration of Hebrew in Roman characters.] Paris, 1964. (NF Z 46-003)
  Follows the ISO/R259 scheme.

438
SCHRAMM, G.M. The graphemes of Tiberian Hebrew. Berkeley, University of California Press, 1964. 68 p.
  A comparative table of transliteration vs. transcription appears on p. 20.

439
OPPENHEIMER, H. [On the question of transliteration.] Yad Lakore, 8, July-Aug. 1967:115-120. (In Hebrew)
  The library of the Hebrew University in Jerusalem will follow the transcription rules of the Academy of the Hebrew language, and will gradually change its Romanized headings accordingly. The rules are reprinted in an appendix.

440
WEINBERG, W. Transliteration and transcription of Hebrew. Hebrew Union College Annual, 40-41, 1969-70:1-32.

The most extensive and scholarly treatment of the problem so far. There are several comparative tables showing the major transliteration and transcription schemes proposed or in use from the Renaissance until 1970. The author proposes a new Romanization scheme which differentiates between "narrow", "broad" and "popular" versions, since more than one scheme is needed for different purposes. There is a glossary of Hebrew words in English spelling, listing about 300 words in the "popular" Romanization.

441
ZAFREN, H.C. Computers, transliterations and related things. In Association of Jewish Libraries [C], 1969, p. 55-56.
A summary of the scheme presented in 421.

442
ENCYCLOPEDIA JUDAICA. Jerusalem, Keter Publ. House, 1972.
The transliteration scheme used is explained in vol. 1, p. 10. It differs from those used in 426, 430 and also from the official Israeli system (432), being a mixture of transliteration and transcription for English-speaking readers.

Hebrew-Greek

443
BERTRAM, G. Das Problem der griechischen Umschrift des hebräischen Alten Testaments. [The problem of the Greek transcription of the Hebrew O.T.] Die Welt des Orients, 5, no. 2, 1970:237-264.

444
EMERTON, J.A. Were Greek transliterations of the Hebrew Old Testament used by Jews before the time of Origen? J. Theol. Stud., 21, April 1970:17-31.
Some passages in the Talmud have been interpreted as indicating that Jewish communities in the 3rd c. A.D. used transliterated Bible texts. This assumption is refuted, since there were rabbinical injunctions against pronouncing Hebrew "in a Greek manner". Origen's Hexapla was probably the first transcription of Hebrew in Greek characters.

Hebrew-Lithuanian

445
KISINAS, I. Nelotyniškųjų abėcėliu transkripcija; Hebrajų. [Non-Roman alphabet transcription; Hebrew.] Bibliografijos Žinios, 10, 1937:28.

Hebrew-Polish

446
NOWICKI, P. O transkrypcji hebraiskich "matres lectionis". [On the transcription of Hebrew "matres lectionis".] Spraw. Posied. Tow. Nauk, Warszaw. Jezyk. Hist. Lit., 42, 1949:167.

Hebrew-Judeo=Arabic

447
SEYBOLD, C.F. Faksimileseite eines Thoramanuscripts auf Pergament in spanischer Quadratschrift mit punktiertem Targûm und Sa'adjâ (in spanisch-arabischer Vulgäraussprache hebräisch vokalisiert) am Rande. [Facsimile page of a Thora-MS on parchment in Spanish square script with pointed Targum and Sa'adya (in Spanish-Arabic popular pronunciation and Hebrew vocalization) in the margin.] In [Festschr. Derenbourg], 1909. p.61-65.

Hebrew-Chinese

448
BEN-ZVI, Y. [The stone tablets of the old synagogue in Kaifeng-fu.] In his [Collected works] Jerusalem, Yad Yizhak Ben-Zvi, 1965. Vol. 2, p. 225-269. (In Hebrew)
   On Chinese phonetic transcriptions of Hebrew names found in the synagogue of a Chinese Jewish community.

449
LESLIE, D. Some notes on the Jewish inscriptions of K'aifeng. J. Amer. Oriental Soc., 82, 1962:346-361.
   More on the same subject, with detailed analysis of the Chinese phonetics involved in the transcriptions of Hebrew names.

***

See also 66, 73, 79, 84, 86, 87, 89, 90, 405, 419-422, 711. Ladino 177-180. Judeo=Arabic 178, 181, 182.

Hebraization

450
BEN YEHUDA, M. [Spelling in the Hebrew catalog.] Yad Lakore, 9, July 1968:85-92. (In Hebrew)
   A set of rules for the Hebraization of names written in other scripts, based on the phonetic transcription of the sound values of the various languages.

See also Italian-Hebrew 184. German-Hebrew 193-195. Arabic-Hebrew 428, 492.

Syriac

See 66, 84, 86, 87, 89, 422, 429.

Arabic

Romanization

451
SMITH, E. A. Essay on the pronunciation of Arabic. B. Lists of Arabic names of places in Palestine. In E. Robinson and E. Smith. Biblical researches in Palestine and in the adjacent regions. Boston, 1841. Appendix 2.
   Contains a transliteration scheme for Arabic characters. In the 2nd ed. of this work (Boston, 1860) Smith's scheme appears in tabular form in vol. 1, p. xiii-xv.

452
LEPSIUS, R. Ueber die arabischen Sprachlaute und deren Umschrift... [On the sounds of the Arabic language and their Romanization.] Abhandl. K. Akad. Wiss. Berlin, 1861:97-152.
   The system is intended mainly for philological purposes, but influenced later attempts at Romanization.

453
REDHOUSE, J.W. An appendix on Arabic transliteration and pronunciation. J. Roy. Asiat. Soc., n.s. 18, 1886:294-322.

454
LYON, H.T. On a proposed method of transliterating the languages written in the Arabic character. J. Roy. Asiat. Soc., 1890:631-638.
   Proposes the use of capital letters to transcribe Arabic consonants. There are two tables, and examples of Arabic text transliterated by the author's method. A rejoinder by F.W. Newman appears under the title "Transliteration" in the volume for 1891, p. 340-343.

455
NICOLAS, L., and I. LÉVY. Essai d'une figuration rationnelle des lettres signes de la langue arabe reproduits en caractères latins. [Attempt at a rational figuration of the letter signs of the Arabic language reproduced by Roman characters.] Revue Tunisienne, 1910:54-63, 306-321, 409-419, 510-521.

456
C., D. and A.R.H. Notes on the transliteration of Arabic names for the 1/M. map. Geogr. J., 49, 1917:141-148.

457
BRITISH ACADEMY. Transliteration of Arabic and Persian. Report of the Committee appointed to draw up a practical scheme for the transliteration into English of words and names belonging to the Nearer East. Proc. Brit. Acad., 8, 1917-18:505-521.

458
GLEICHEN, E. The decisions of the Permanent Committee on Geographical Names on the transliteration of Arabic characters. Geogr. J., 56, Oct. 1920:308-313.

459
BRUX, A.A. Arabic-English transliteration for library purposes. Amer. J. Semit. Lang. Lit., 47, Oct. 1930. Supplement. 30 p.
   Examines 24 different transliteration and transcription schemes and discusses their various features from the point of view of bibliographical control. Has a comparative table of all 24 schemes. Brux favours transliteration, since pronunciation of Arabic varies widely, thus making transcription impractical.

460
PALESTINE. GOVERNMENT. Transliteration from Arabic and Hebrew into English, from Arabic into Hebrew, and from Hebrew into Arabic, with transliterated lists of personal and geographical names for use in Palestine. Jerusalem, Goldberg's Press, 1931. 85 p.
   Issued by the Palestine Government as its official code of transliteration.

461
MIELI, A., H.P.J. RENAUD and F. TAESCHNER. La transcription en lettres latines des mots arabes. [The transcription of Arabic words in Roman characters.] Archeion, 14, 1932: 436-444.

462
BROCKELMANN, C., et al. Vorschlag eines internationalen Transkriptionssystems für die islamischen Literatursprachen, der Deutschen Morgenländischen Gesellschaft vorgelegt von C. Brockelmann ... [Proposal for an international system of transcription for the Islamic literary languages, etc.] Halle, 1933.

463
DANIŞMAN, N. Transcription de l'alphabet arabe. [Transcription of the Arabic alphabet.] Revue des Etudes Islamiques, 9, 1935:97-103.
   Proposes new letter forms for sounds not represented by Roman characters, with a view to future Latinization of Arabic. He mentions that there are more than 2000 different schemes, tables or proposals for the Romanization of Arabic.

464
MIELI, A. Observations sur la transcription des mots arabes. [Observations on the transcription of Arabic words.] Archeion, 17, 1935:412-413.

465
RUSKA, J. Die Umschrift des arabischen Alphabets nach den Beschlüssen des XIX. Internationalen Orientalisten Kongresses in Rom. [The transcription of the Arabic alphabet according to the resolutions of the 19th International Congress of Orientalists in Rome.] Archeion, 17, 1935:410-412.

466
TAESCHNER, F. Die Transliteration der arabischen Schrift. [The transliteration of the Arabic script.] Actes Congr. Int. Orient., 19e, Rome, 1935:555-556.

467
PAXTON, E.H. A suggestion for the transliteration of the Arabic language. Bull. Faculty of Arts, Cairo University, 4, 1936:131-136.

468
FAHMI, A. [Roman characters for the writing of Arabic.] Cairo, 1944. (In Arabic)

469
MALZAC, A.G. Alphabet occidental pour transcrire l'arabe. [A Western alphabet for the transcription of Arabic.] Actes Congr. Int. Orient., 21e, Paris, 1948: 287-289.

470
THYS, E. Poging tot transcriptie van de arabische eigennamen. [An attempt at transcribing Arabic personal names.] Biblioteeksgids, 29, Nov.-Dec. 1953:122-125.
   On the confusion in this field, mainly caused by the differences between colloquial and written language. Considers Brockelmann's scheme (see 462) the best guide. A list of several dozen Arabic names in transcription is appended.

471
WICKENS, G.M. The transliteration of Arabic, an approach in the light of current problems of printing and publication. J. Near Eastern Studies, 12, 1953:253-256.

471a
PAREJA, F.M. Los problemas de la transliteración. In his Islamología. Madrid, Razon y Fe, 1952-54, vol. 1, p. 8-11.
   Discusses the difficulties involved in transliteration of Arabic names, with particular reference to Spanish. There is a comparative table of transliteration schemes showing the ISO system and English, French, German, Spanish, Italian, Dutch and Russian variations found in the respective literatures.

472
KAFAFI, M. Hoover Institute and Library; Arabic transliteration. Stanford, Calif., Hoover Institute and Library, 1956.
   Also published in Arabic in 'Alam al-Maktabat, 1, 1959: 69-73.

473
PARÉJA, F.M. The problems of Arabic transliteration. Actes Congr. Int. Orient., 22e, 1951. Vol. 2 (1957):134-137.

474
SPALDING, C.S. An Arabic transliteration table and manual. Library of Congress Information Bull., 17, Sept. 22, 1958: 541-542.

475
INTERNATIONAL ORGANIZATION FOR STANDARDIZATION. International system for the transliteration of Arabic characters. Geneva, 1961. 8 p. (ISO/R233).

476
HERMELINK, H., and E.S. KENNEDY. Transcription of Arabic letters in geometric figures. J. Amer. Orient. Soc., 82, 1962:204.
   Proposes "simple" transliteration of Arabic letters appearing in medieval mathematical works.

477
ASSOCIATION FRANÇAISE DE NORMALISATION. Translittération des caractères arabes en caractères latins. [Transliteration of Arabic characters into Latin characters.] Paris, 1963. (NF Z 46-002)
   Follows the ISO/R233 scheme.

478
LADEFROUX, M. Recommendation ISO/R233. Système international pour la translittération des caractères arabes. [The recommendation ISO/R233. An international system for the transliteration of Arabic characters.] Courrier de la Normalisation, 30, 1963:55-56.

479
EL-HADI, M.M. Arabic library resources in the United States. Urbana, Ill., University of Illinois, 1964. (Ph.D. thesis)
   Transliteration: p. 156-165.

480
RODINSON, M. Les principes de la translittération, la translittération de l'arabe et la nouvelle norme de l'ISO. [Principles of transliteration, the transliteration of Arabic and the new ISO standard.] Bull. Bibl. France, 9, 1964:1-24.
   A critical evaluation of 475 in the light of general principles of transliteration and transcription.

481
WARD, P. [Letter to the editor.] J. Docum., 21, 1965:199-200.
   On the transliteration of Arabic, with proposals for a "uniform" scheme, as opposed to the ISO/R233 scheme which is rejected as ambiguous and not suitable for typing.

482
AMAN, M.M. Analysis of terminology, form and structure of subject headings in Arabic literature, and formulation of rules for Arabic subject headings. Pittsburgh, University of Pittsburgh, 1968. (Ph.D. thesis)
   Chapter 9. Transliteration and filing integration, deals with the complexities of transliteration of Arabic, particularly in library catalogs.

483
BRITISH STANDARDS INSTITUTION. British standard for the transliteration of Arabic characters. London, 1968. 7 p. (B.S. 4280:1968)
   Follows ISO/R233, except for ﺝ (ñ, not g).

484
LIBRARY OF CONGRESS. Arabic Romanization. Cataloging Service, Bull. 91, Sept. 1970. 8 p.
   Supersedes the table in ALA Cataloging Rules, p. 248 (90) and the scheme published in LC's Bull. 49 (1958).

485
WHEELER, G. The transliteration of Arabic script. Asian Affairs, 58, 1971:317-320.

486
AMERICAN NATIONAL STANDARDS INSTITUTE. System for the Romanization of Arabic. New York, 1972. (ANSI Z39.12-1972)
   Virtually identical with the LC scheme.

Arabic-Portuguese

487
MACHADO, J.P. A transcrição portuguesa do alfabeto arábico. [On the Portuguese transcription of the Arabic alphabet.] Soc. Geogr. Lisboa Bol., 79, 1961:355-360.

Arabic-French

488
HUART, C. Transcription des semi-voyelles y, w, redoublées en arabe. [Transcription of the semi-vowels y, w, doubled in Arabic.] Mém. Soc. Ling. Paris, 13, 1905-06:411-412.

489
FRANCE. ARMÉE. ETAT MAJOR. COMMANDEMENT SUPÉRIEUR DES TROUPES DU LEVANT. Règles de transcription des noms arabes & vocabulaires arabe-français & turc-français. [Rules for transcription of Arabic names and Arabic-French and Turkish-French vocabularies.] Beyrouth, 1945.

490
CAILLEMER, A. Vocabulaire arabe-français et règles de correspondance pour servir à la transcription des toponymes arabes. [Arabic-French vocabulary and rules of correspondence for the transcription of Arabic place names.] Paris, Institut géographique national, 1954. 285 p.

Arabic-Italian

491
INEICHEN, G. La traslitterazione dei termini arabi e la stratificazione degli arabismi nel Medio Evo. [The transliteration of Arabic terms and the stratification of Arabisms in the Middle Ages.] Boll. dell'Atlante linguistico mediterraneo, 8/9, 1966-67:197-203.

Arabic-German

492
BRAUN, H. Die alphabetische Katalogisierung von Werken in arabischer, persischer und türkischer Sprache. [The alphabetical cataloging of works in the Arabic, Persian and Turkish language.] Z. Bibl. Bibliogr., 11, Nr. 1, 1964:9-32.
   A thorough examination of the problems of transliteration of Arabic, Persian and Ottoman Turkish as encountered in German library practice, and with reference to the ISO/R233 transliteration standard.

Arabic-Bulgarian

493
NEDKOV, B. [On the correct spelling of Arabic place names and personal names.] Bălgarski Ezik, 13, 1963:138-141. (In Bulgarian)

Arabic-Hebrew

494
ISRAEL. MINISTRY OF INTERIOR. MINORITIES DEPARTMENT. [Rules for transliteration from Arabic to Hebrew and for the listing of Arabic names.] Jerusalem, 1966. 11 p. (In Hebrew)

Arabic-Georgian

495
MEGRELIDZE, I.V. [The Arabic alphabet in Old Georgian transcription.] Epigrafika Vostoka, 8, 1953:36-42. (In Russian)

***

See also 66, 77, 84, 86, 87, 89-92, 391-394, 401, 403-405, 412, 414, 419, 420. Place names 711, 721, 722, 742.

Arabization of Roman script

496
ENGELBACH, R. Some suggestions on the transcription of European words into the Arabic alphabet. Bull. de l'Institut français d'archéologie orientale, 32, 1932:1-6.

***

See also Kurdish-Arabic script 657, 658. French-Arabic script 183, 183a. Polish-Arabic script 289a. Serbian-Arabic script 278, 278a, 278b. Ukrainian-Arabic script 367. Chinese-Arabic script 657, 658, 658a. African languages-Arabic script 638.

Judeo=Arabic

See 178, 181-182a, 447.

Amharic

497
LIBRARY OF CONGRESS. Romanization system for Amharic. Cataloging Service, Bull. 104, April 1972:14-20.

See also 66, 84, 86, 87, 89, 711.

Coptic

See 66, 84, 87, 89, 422.

V. CAUCASIAN LANGUAGES

Georgian

Romanization

Georgian-Hungarian

498
MOLNÁR, N. Az örmény és gruz cimek átirásáról. [On the transliteration of Armenian and Georgian entries.] Magyar Könyvszemle, 80, 1964:181-183.

***

See also 84, 87, 172. Arabic-Georgian 493.

Cyrillization

499
DANELIA, S. [On the question of Russian transcriptions of certain groups of Georgian family names.] Izv. Akad. Nauk SSSR, Otd. Lit. Jaz., 1950:402-405. (In Russian)

500
KIBRIK, A.E., and S.V. KODZASOV. [Principles of phonetic transcription and the system of transcription of Caucasian languages.] Voprosy Jazykoznanija, no. 6, 1970:66-78. (In Russian)

VI. LANGUAGES OF EURASIA AND NORTHERN ASIA

URALIAN LANGUAGES

Finnish

See 365, 388.

Hungarian

501
FISCHER, K.A. A hun-magyar irás és annak fennmarodt emlékei. (Tizenkét régi magyar alphabettel és 83 különféle ábrával.) [The Hunnic-Magyarian script and its remaining residues (12 old Hungarian alphabets and 83 various comparisons.)] Budapest, 1889. 105 p.
   A study of the Hungarian and Hunnic alphabets with tables of comparison and transcription.

***

See also Armenian-Hungarian 153. Cyrillic-Hungarian 267-271. Macedonian-Hungarian 275. White=Russian-Hungarian 368. Cyrillization of names 388. Georgian-Hungarian 498. Chinese-Hungarian 650, 651.

ALTAIC LANGUAGES

Turkish (Osmanli)

Latinization

502
BOLLAND, W. Schriftreform in der Türkei. [Reform of the script in Turkey.] Mitt. Seminars Orientalische Sprachen, 31, 1928:70-90.

503
JUZBAŠEV, N. [The Arabic and the new Turkish alphabet.] Kul'tura i Pismennost' Vostoka, 1, 1928:65-69. (In Russian)

504
La réforme de l'alphabet turc. [The reform of the Turkish alphabet.] Correspondence d'Orient, 20, 1928:219-221.

505
WOOD, M.M. Latinizing the Turkish alphabet. Amer. J. Sociol., 35, 1929-30:194-203.

506
WEISSBACH, F.H. Die türkische Lateinschrift. [The Turkish Roman script.] Archiv für Schreib- und Buchwesen, 4, 1930: 125-138.
   Reprinted in 22.

507
L'Adoption des caractères latins en Turquie en 1928. [The adoption of Roman characters in Turkey in 1928.] Ankara, Millî Eğitim Basımevi, 1951. 20 p.
   An official Turkish account of the Latinization.

508
KONONOV, A.N. [The reform of the alphabet in Turkey; on the history of the question.] Učenje Zapiski Leningrad. Univ., 1959:158-169. (In Russian)

***

See also 29.

Romanization

509
FOY, K. Die ältesten osmanischen Transscriptionstexte in gothischen Lettern. [The oldest Ottomanic texts transcribed in black letter.] Mitt. Semin. Orient. Sprach., Abt. 2: Westasiat. Stud., 4, 1902:230-277; 5, 1903:233-293.
   On a transliteration of parts of Turkish texts in the Tractatus de moribus Turcorum (Urach, C. Fyner, 1481)

510
HEFFENING, W. Die türkischen Transkriptionstexte des Bartholomaeus Georgievits aus den Jahren 1544-1548; ein Beitrag zur historischen Grammatik des Osmanisch-Türkischen. [The

Turkish texts transcribed by Bartholomaeus Georgievits from 1544 to 1548; a contribution to the historical grammar of Ottoman Turkish.] Leipzig, Deutsche Morgenländische Gesellschaft, 1942. 124 p.
   A bibliography of transcribed Turkish texts, p. 3-11.

511
BOMBACI, A. Recenti edizioni di testi turchi in trascrizione. [Recent editions of transcribed Turkish texts.] Oriente Moderno, 29, 1949:176-189.

512
WEIL, G. Ein unbekannter türkischer Transkriptionstext aus dem Jahre 1489. [An unknown Turkish transcribed text from the year 1489.] Oriens, 6, 1953:239-265.
   On a few lines of Turkish text, transliterated by Roman characters, in Petrus de Brutis' work (see 423a). This is one of the earliest known transliterations of Turkish.

513
BRAUN, H. Die alphabetische Katalogisierung von Werken in arabischer, persischer und türkischer Sprache. [The alphabetical cataloging of works in the Arabic, Persian and Turkish language.] Z. Bibl. Bibliogr., 11, Nr. 1, 1964:9-32.

514
BIRNBAUM, E. Transliteration of Ottoman Turkish for library and general purposes. J. Amer. Orient. Soc., 87, 1967:122-156.
   An extensive treatment of the subject, with many examples of names and texts in Ottoman Turkish. The transliteration scheme for Arabic script used by the Library of Congress covers all languages written in Arabic script except Ottoman Turkish. The author proposes his own scheme which has already been adopted by the catalogers of the British Museum.

***

See also 66, 84, 87, 89, 91, 92, 392, 394.

Cyrillization

515
HAZAI, G. Ein kyrillischer Transkriptionstext des Türkischen. [A Turkish text transcribed into Cyrillic.] Studia Slavica Academiae Scientiarum Hungaricae, 12, 1966:173-179.
   On an Ottoman Turkish version of the Credo in Cyrillic script, edited in Damascus in the 19th century.

Other Turkic languages

Latinization

516
CASTAGNÉ, J.A. La latinisation de l'alphabet turk dans les républiques turkotatares de l'URSS. [The Latinization of the Turkic alphabet in the Turko-Tataric republics of the

USSR.] <u>Revue d'Etudes Islamiques</u>, 1927:321-353.

517
CASTAGNÉ, J.A. Le mouvement de latinisation dans les républiques soviétiques musulmanes et les pays voisins (documents de presse russe). [The movement of Latinization in the Islamic Soviet republics and in neighbouring countries (documents from the Russian press).] <u>Revue d'Etudes Islamiques</u>, 1928:559-595.

518
IMART, G. Le mouvement de "Latinisation" en U.R.S.S. [The movement of "Latinization" in the U.S.S.R.] <u>Cahiers du Monde Russe et Soviétique</u>, <u>6</u>, 1965:223-239.
   An historical survey of the Latinization movement, particularly for the Turkic and Mongolian languages, and its demise after World War II.

***

See also 28, 743.

Romanization

519
RICHTER, Erich. Zur bibliothekarischen Transkription der kyrillischen Buchstaben einiger finnisch-ugrischer Sprachen in der Sovietunion. [On the bibliographical transliteration of Cyrillic characters of some Finno-Ugric languages in the Soviet Union.] <u>Ural-Altaische Jahrbücher</u>, <u>31</u>, 1959:344-346.
   How to transcribe the additional characters added to the Cyrillic alphabet for some languages in the Soviet Union when such entries have to be integrated into transliterated German library catalogs.

520
NAGY, E. Transzliterálási problémák a Szovjetunió finnugor nyelveinéi. [Problems of transliteration in connection with Finno-Ugric languages of the Soviet Union.] <u>Magyar Könyvszemle</u>, <u>80</u>, 1964:374-379.

Cyrillization

521
BASKAKOV, N.A. [The present state of scripts for Turkic languages in the U.S.S.R. and their future improvement.] <u>Voprosy Jazykoznanija</u>, no. 5, 1967:33-46. (In Russian)
   A proposal for a unified alphabet, suitable for all Turkic languages in the Soviet Union. It is based on the Cyrillic alphabet and contains 42 characters.

522
SIGORSKIJ, M.D. On the question of transcribing authors' names in the Turkic languages of the U.S.S.R.] <u>Sovetskaja Bibliografija</u>, <u>2</u>, 1934:98-128. (In Russian)

***

See also 229.

Mongolian

Romanization

523
POPPE, N. Vorschläge zu einer einheitlichen mongolistischen Transkription. [Proposals for a unified Mongolistic transcription.] Ural-Altaische Jahrbücher, 25, 1953:119-132.

See also 711.

Transcription into Chinese characters

524
LIGETI, L. Transcriptions chinoises de trois noms propres dans l'Histoire secrète des Mongols. [Chinese transcription of three proper names in the "Secret history of the Mongols"] In [Festschr. Rintchen], 1966. p. 123-136.

Manchu

525
LANGLÈS, L.M. Alphabet Mantchou, rédigée d'après le syllabaire et le dictionnaire universel de cette langue ... [The Manchu alphabet, edited according to the syllabary and the universal dictionary of that language ...] 3e éd. Paris, 1807. xv, 208 p.

526
SINOR, D. La transcription du Mandjou. [The transcription of Manchu.] Journal Asiatique, 1949:261-272.

Korean

Romanization

527
ASTON, W.G. Writing, printing and the alphabet in Corea. J. Roy. Asiat. Soc., 1895:505-511.

528
McCUNE, G.M., and E.O. REISCHAUER. Romanization of the Korean language. Trans. Roy. Asiat. Soc., Korean Branch, 29, 1939:1-55.

529
AMERICAN LIBRARY ASSOCIATION. Manual of Romanization, capitalization, punctuation and word division for Chinese, Japanese and Korean. In its Cataloging rules of the American Library Association and the Library of Congress; additions and changes, 1949-1958. Washington, D.C., Library of Congress, 1959. p. 56.

***

See also 77. Place names, 711, 723.

Cyrillization

530
VĂGLENOV, M., and I. KANČEV. [Pronunciation and transcription of Korean names in Bulgarian.] Bălgarski Ezik, 19, 1969:280-287. (In Bulgarian)

Transliteration into Chinese characters

531
OGURA, S. [Translation of Korean into Chinese.] [n.p.] 1958. (In Japanese)

Transliteration into Korean characters

532
HAN'GUI, H. [Unification of Koreanized foreign words.] Seoul, 1941. (In Korean)

See also 660, 661.

Japanese

Romanization

533
ROMAJI FUKYU KAI. A short statement of the aim and method of the Rōmāji Kai. Tokyo, 1885. 28 p.

534
AXON, E. Classification and cataloguing: Japanese names. Library Association Record, 20, 1918:231-232.

535
TANAKADATE, A. Circumstances of introducing Roman characters to Japanese writing. Bull. des Rélations Scientifiques, 3, 1928:1-16.

536
PIERSON, J.L. On the transliteration and transcription of the Japanese Kana, archaic, ancient and modern. Asiatic Society of Japan Trans., ser. 2, 6, 1929:103-144.

537
PALMER, H.E. The principles of Romanization, with special reference to the romanization of Japanese. Tokyo, Maruzen, 1931. v, 157 p.

538
ROMAJI HIROME KAI. The Japanese language and the Roman alphabet; a short statement of the Japanese standard system. Tokyo, 1931. 14 p.

539
HATSUKADE, I. Die Reform der japanischen Nationalschrift. Geschichte der Reformbestrebungen. [The reform of the Japanese national script; history of the reform movements.] Gutenberg-Jahrbuch, 7, 1932:27-43.
   Traces the attempts at Romanizing and reform of the Japanese script from the 16th century to the late 1920'ies. Shows several examples of Romanized Japanese texts.

540
JIMBO, K. The question of writing the Japanese language with the Roman letters. Tokyo, Romaji-Hirome-Kai, 1933. 34 p.

541
SOMERVILLE, J.C. The phonetic transliteration of Japanese: a plea for the retention of the Hepburn system. Trans. Proc. Japan Soc., 31, 1934:79-94.

542
MAMIYA, F. [Library catalogs and the system of Roman spelling.] Toshokan Kenkyū, 9, 1936:543-547. (In Japanese)

543
MATTICE, H.A. Japanese books in American libraries. Libr. Quart., 8, 1938:13-24.
  On the need for Romanizing Japanese entries in American catalogs. Displays an extreme xenophobic view, denying to Chinese and Japanese people any understanding of the problem as seen by an American librarian.

544
CARR, D. New official Romanization of Japanese. J. Amer. Orient. Soc., 59, March 1939:99-102.
  Urges the adoption of the then recently introduced Kokutei-shiki system (which is based on phonemic transcription, whereas the Hepburn system is a phonetic one).

545
FUKUDA, N. Some problems in cataloging Japanese books for American libraries. Ann Arbor, University of Michigan, 1940.
  Unpublished Master's thesis. Investigates the difficulties involved in establishing the correct forms of entry for Japanese names, particularly those from the pre-Meiji period. The problem of Japanese corporate names is also discussed.

546
REISCHAUER, E.O. Romaji or Romazi. J. Amer. Orient. Soc., 60, March 1940:82-89.
  A refutation of Carr's arguments (see 544) and a defense of the Hepburn system as against the Kokutei-shiki system. For bibliographical purposes, the phonetic system is preferable.

547
CARR, D. Japanese Romanization again. J. Amer. Orient. Soc., 61, Sept. 1941:188-190.
  A rebuttal to 546. The Japanese attack on Pearl Harbor a few months after the publication of this article seems to have silenced any further discussion of the topic until the early 1950'ies.

548
TAMARU, T. [Research on Romanized sentences.] 4th ed. Tokyo, 1942. (In Japanese)

549
JONES, D. The Romanization of Japanese. Z. Phonet. allgem. Sprachwiss., 3, 1949:68-74.

550
SUPREME COMMANDER FOR THE ALLIED POWERS. CIVIL INFORMATION AND EDUCATION SECTION. The development and present status of Romaji in Japan. Tokyo, 1950. 42 p.

551
UNITED STATES. ARMY LANGUAGE SCHOOL. Romaji (Hepburn system). Presidio of Monterey, Army Language School, Japanese Language Dept., 1950. 10 p.

552
MISH, J.L. The transliteration of Oriental languages in chemical literature. J. Chem. Educ., 32, March 1955:137-138.
  On the differences between the Japanese transliteration system and the Hepburn system used in the Western world, particularly as this affects the spelling of personal names and chemical substances. Some examples from Chinese and Arabic are also discussed.

553
CH'EN, CH'ING-CHIN. [Selected works on the history of the reform of the Japanese language.] Peking, 1957. 90 p. (In Chinese)
  Discusses also the transliteration and Romanization movements.

554
AMERICAN LIBRARY ASSOCIATION. Manual of Romanization, capitalization, punctuation and word division for Chinese, Japanese and Korean. In its Cataloging rules of the American Library Association and the Library of Congress; additions and changes, 1949-1958. Washington, D.C., Library of Congress, 1959. p. 48-56.

555
HORIUCHI, Y. [Word-by-word division of Japanese sentences written in Romanized Japanese; practical dictionary.] Tokyo, 1959. 141 p. (In Japanese)

555a
HORIUCHI, Y. [How to divide Japanese sentences word by word.] Tokyo, 1960. 280 p. (In Japanese)

556
SEITZ, R.O. Japlish, the Japanese brand of English. Special Libraries, 53, Jan. 1962:30-34.

557
TSUKAMOTO, J.T. A study of problems of Romanization of the Japanese language in library cataloging. Austin, University of Texas, 1962.

Unpublished Master's thesis. Summarizes the history of various Romanization schemes and discusses the difficulties in establishing a Romanized form of Japanese names. There are comparative tables of the Japanese syllables as Romanized by the Hepburn, Nippon-shiki and Kokutei-shiki systems.

558
MATSUMURA, T. Word division in romanized Japanese titles. Chicago, University of Chicago, 1964. ii, 198 l. Unpublished Master's thesis.

559
MIYAZAKI, S. [The Japanese people and Romanization.] Tokyo, Romaji Kai, 1964. 62 p. (In Japanese)

560
HIROMATSU, H. [Why Romanization?] Kotobano Kyoiku, 1965: 1-3. (In Japanese)

561
BABA, S. [Bibliographical Romanization of non-Roman characters.] Tokyo, 1968. 433 p. (In Japanese)

Japanese-English

562
CH'EN, C.K.H. A standard romanized dictionary of Chinese and Japanese popular surnames. Hanover, N.H., Oriental Society, 1972. 681 p.

Japanese-German

563
TRAUTZ, F.M. Zur "Transkriptionsfrage" der japanischen und der chinesischen Schrift. [On the "question of transcription" of the Japanese and Chinese script.] Ostasiatische Rundschau, 9, 1927:102-104, 127-130.

564
SCHARSCHMIDT, C. Zur "Transkriptionsfrage" der japanischen Schrift. [On the "question of transcription" of the Japanese script.] Ostasiatische Rundschau, 9, 1928:185-190.

565
HENKEL, R. Die deutsche Umschrift. [The German transcription ⟨i.e. of the Japanese script⟩.] Nippon, 5, 1939:103-111.

566
LÖHR, H. Transliteration japanischer Wörter über die kyrillische in die lateinische Schrift. [Transcription of Japanese words into Roman script via the Cyrillic.] Informatik, 18, Nr. 5, 1971:48-52.
   Because of the syllabic structure of Japanese, the form of words transliterated from Japanese directly into Roman differs from the same words transliterated into Roman script via the Cyrillic; this occurs when citations in

the Russian Referativnyj Žurnal are re-processed for Western information systems which contain Japanese citations transliterated directly, and has very serious consequences for retrieval. A concordance list of Japanese syllables in direct Romanization and in Cyrillization is given as an aid for conversion.

***

See also 22, 77, 602, 638, 711, 749.

Cyrillization

567
VĂGLENOV, M. [Pronunciation and transcription of Japanese names in Bulgarian.] Bǎlgarski Ezik, 18, 1968:54-63. (In Bulgarian)

Transcription into Japanese characters

568
[Transcription of the non-Roman character foreign languages.] Toshokan Kenkyu, 10, 1937:1-11. (In Japanese)

VII. DRAVIDIAN LANGUAGES

Kannada

569
LIBRARY OF CONGRESS. [Transliteration of] Kannada. Cataloging Service, Bull. 64, Feb. 1964. p. 7.

See also 13, 122.

Tamil

570
LIBRARY OF CONGRESS. [Transliteration of] Tamil. Cataloging Service, Bull. 64, Feb. 1964. p. 13.

571
RAJAGOPALACHARI, C. Romanizing Tamil words. Swaragya, May 1968:1-2.

572
SUBBIAH, R. Transliteration of Tamil - a new system. In Intern. Conf. Seminar Tamil Studies [C], 1968-69. Vol. 2, p. 644-649.

See also 13, 82, 115. Place names 724.

Malayalam

573
LIBRARY OF CONGRESS. [Transcription of] Malayalam. Cataloging Service, Bull. 64, Feb. 1964. p. 8.

See also 13, 66, 82, 84, 87, 414.

Telugu

574
LIBRARY OF CONGRESS. [Transliteration of] Telugu. Cataloging Service, Bull. 64, Feb. 1964. p. 14.

See also 13.

VIII. LANGUAGES OF SOUTH-EAST ASIA

Sino-Tibetan languages

Chinese

Romanization

575
SCHÜTZ, F. Propagation des sciences européennes dans l'Extrême Orient. Nouveau syllabaire et alphabet chinois phonétique. Transcription chinois de tous les noms étrangers, et correction des traductions de la Bible. [Propagation of European sciences in the Far East. New syllabary and Chinese phonetic alphabet. Chinese transcription of all foreign names and correction to Bible translations.] Nancy, Grimblot & Raybois, 1856-57. 2 v.

576
WADE, T. Yü-yên tzŭ-êrh chi ... a progressive course designed to assist the student of colloquial Chinese. London, Trübner, 1867.
   Contains Wade's transcription scheme, later simplified by Giles (see 578) and known as the "Wade-Giles system".

577
ZOTTOLI, A. Cursus litteraturae sinicae. [A course in Chinese literature.] Chang-hai, 1879-80. 4 v.
   Uses his own transcription system into Latin.

578
GILES, H.A. A Chinese-English dictionary. London, B. Quaritch, 1892.
   Introduced the simplification of Wade's system (see 576).

579
LEAMAN, C. General romanization of the Mandarin dialect. Nanking, 1897.

580
EDUCATIONAL ASSOCIATION OF CHINA. The standard system of Mandarin romanization; introduction, sound table, and syllabary. Shanghai, 1904.

581
HIRTH, F. Umschreibung chinesischer Schriftzeichen in dem für Schriftzwecke modifizierten Dialekt von Peking. [Transcription of Chinese characters in the Peking dialect, modi-

fied for writing purposes.] In Internationaler Orientalisten-Kongress. 13th, Hamburg, 1902. Verhandlungen. Leiden, 1904. p. 177-186.
   A proposal for an "international" system of transcription. It was not accepted by the Congress which instead recommended "national" systems, based on the spelling and pronunciation used in the vernaculars of different countries.

582
KARLGREN, B. The romanization of Chinese. London, China Society, 1928. 12 p.

583
SIMON, W. Chinesisch. [Chinese <i.e. characters>.] In Lautzeichen und ihre Anwendung, etc. [C], 1928. p. 96-104.

584
WANG, CHIN CHUN. The new phonetic system of writing Chinese characters. Chinese Social and Political Science Rev., 13, 1929:144-160.

585
CH'I, T'IEH-HEN. [Transliteration of Chinese] Gwoyeu Romatzyh, Chyitieehenn bianjih, Fangyih jiawding. Shanghai, 1930. 39 p. (In Chinese)
   (The transcribed title actually appears in this form on the title page after the Chinese title.)

586
SCHUBERT, J. Lateinschrift oder Nationalschrift in China. [Roman script or national script in China.] Archiv für Schreib- und Buchwesen, 4, 1930:145-148.
   Reprinted in 22.

587
WICHNER, F. Lateinschrift in China. [Roman script in China.] Archiv für Schreib- und Buchwesen, 4, 1930:149-160.
   Reprinted in 22.

588
GARDNER, C.S. The Western transcription of Chinese. J. N. China Br. Roy. Asiat. Soc., 62, 1931:137-147.

589
WARE, J.R. Transliteration of the names of Chinese Buddhist monks. J. Amer. Orient. Soc., 52, June 1932:159-162.

590
T'AN, JUNG-KUANG. [Dictionary of Cantonese phonetic spelling.] Hong-Kong, 1934. 42 p. (In Chinese)

591
CHIANG, CHING-FU. [Transliteration of Chinese.] Kunming, 1941. 51 p. (In Chinese)

592
Chinese written phonetically. Books Abroad, 15, Oct. 1941: 422-423.

593
WANG, CHIN CHUN. Hsin hanzyx (phonetic Chinese). <u>Chinese Social and Political Science Review</u>, 24, Oct. 1940-Jan. 1941:263-290A; 453-456.

594
WERNER, E.T.C. A suggestion for the compilation of an alphabetical Chinese-English dictionary. Shanghai, Shanghai Times, 1941. 80 p.

595
SIMON, W. The new official Chinese-Latin script, Gwoyen Romatzyh. Tables, rules, illustrative examples. London, Probsthain, 1942. 63 p.

596
CORTA, J.F. De latinisatione linguae sinensis. [On the Latinization of the Chinese language.] <u>Collectanea Commissionis Synodalis</u>, 14, 1941:989-1005; 1130-1142; 15, 1942:188-205; 16, 1943:376-386; 489-509.
   An historical survey of 50 years' work towards a Romanization of Chinese script.

597
DE FRANCIS, J. The alphabetization of Chinese. <u>J. Amer. Oriental Soc.</u>, 43, 1943:225-240.
   On the need for an alphabetical Chinese script, the various attempts at creating such a script, and the problems involved.

598
[The system of Romanization of the Chinese language.] Shanghai, 1944. 93 p. (In Chinese)

599
CHOU, PIEN-MING. Internationalizing the Chinese script: progress in quokyu romanization 1937-45. Bat nyan kangjann jonquok yuwen quokdsih-huah di dsinnjaan: Q. R. 1937-45, by Jou Bienming. Amoy, College of Arts, National University of Amoy, 1945. 1 v.
   Another system of Romanization. Note the difference in the spelling of the author's name in this system as compared to Wade-Giles transcription used by the Library of Congress.

600
LU, CHIN. Chinese-English-French dictionary, featuring a modern practical Chinese script, by Luc Kynh. [n.p.] 1945. xxii, 702 p.
   The author's own system of transcription, which also results in a different spelling of his own name.

601
BOODBERG, P.A. UCI: an interim system of transcription for Chinese. Berkeley, University of California Press, 1947. (California Publ. in East Asiatic Philology, vol. 1, no. 1)

602
BOODBERG, P.A. UCI: an orthographic system of notation and transcription for Sino-Japanese. Berkeley, University of California Press, 1947. (California Publ. in East Asiatic Philology, vol. 1, no. 2)

603
NI, HAI-SHU. [History of Chinese phonetic language movements.] Shanghai, 1948. 229 p. (In Chinese)

604
NI, HAI-SHU. [The rebirth of the Chinese language: essays on the movement for Romanization of Chinese.] Latinxua zhungguoz yndung 20 nian lunwenzi. Shanghai, 1949. 581 p. (In Chinese)

605
DE FRANCIS, J. Nationalism and language reform in China. Princeton, Princeton University Press, 1950. xi, 306 p.
  Deals exhaustively with the various Romanization movements (see also the same author's work 597). A bibliography on Romanization of Chinese is on p. 283-296. For a critical review, see 609.

606
LIN, T'AO. Dingshinghua sin wenz. [New Romanization of the Chinese language.] Peking, 1950. 8, 17, 40 p. (In Chinese)
  The Romanized title is so given on the title page, followed by the Chinese title (here translated) in simplified Chinese characters.

607
BARNETT, K.M.A. A transcription for Cantonese. Bull. Sch. Orient. Afr. Stud., 13, pt. 3, 1951:725-745.

608
HOPE, E.R. Linguistic psychology and the Romanization of Chinese. Ottawa, 1951. 121 p.

609
DUYVENDAK, J.J.L. "John de Francis, 'Nationalism and language reform in China'". T'oung Pao, 41, 1952:234-245.
  See also 605.

610
T'AN, JUNG-KUANG. A new phonetic alphabet for the Cantonese dialect of the Chinese language, by Tam Wing Kwong (Tsam Weing Guong). Hong Kong, Yan Sang Printing Press, 1953. 28 p.
  Note that this author gives his name in two different Romanizations, and that his name is found in the Library of Congress catalog in a third form (Wade-Giles system).

611
UNITED STATES. ARMY LANGUAGE SCHOOL. Romanization list. Presidio of Monterey, Army Language School, Chinese-Mandarin Dept., 1953. 16 p.

612
KUEI, CHUNG-SHU. Kwei's system for the romanization of Chinese. New Haven, 1954. 10 l.

613
PO CHIA HSING. [Standard phonetic spelling of Chinese surnames and "Ch'ien tzŭ wen" in English.] Standard phonetic of Pa chia shing, Chien tzu wen in English. Hong Kong, 1955. 90 p.
   The Chinese title (here translated) is followed by the English title, including the Romanized Chinese words, on the title page. The "Ch'ien tzŭ wen" is an ancient book used as a primer in elementary schools and containing 1000 different characters, not one of which is repeated.

614
HSIA, TAO-TAI China's language reforms. New Haven, Yale University, Institute of Far Eastern Languages, 1956. 200 p.
   Part 2 is entitled "New Latinization Plan" and discusses the 30-letter Roman alphabet promulgated by the Chinese government in 1956. Tables on p. 132-140.

615
UNITED STATES. ARMY COMMAND RECONNAISSANCE ACTIVITIES, PACIFIC (FIELD). Comparative tables of the Wade-Giles and Chinese Communist systems of romanizing Chinese. [n.p.] 1958. 11 l.

616
[Collection of discussions of draft proposals on Chinese phonetic spelling.] Peking, 1957-58. 4 v. (In Chinese)
   Vol. 4 has an added title in Romanized Chinese: Hanyu pinyin fang'an cao'an taolunji.

617
ULVING, T. The transcription of Cantonese; a critical review of some current systems of "tonal spelling", and a presentation of a new national transcription. T'oung Pao, 46, 1958:81-110.
   The author reviews existing systems and proposals and submits his own Romanization scheme.

618
AMERICAN LIBRARY ASSOCIATION. Manual of Romanization, capitalization, punctuation and word division for Chinese, Japanese and Korean. In Cataloging rules of the American Library Association and the Library of Congress; additions and changes, 1949-1958. Washington, D.C., Library of Congress, 1959. p. 47.
   States briefly that the Wade-Giles system is used and gives a few rules of application. Partially superseded and augmented by 624.

619
COHEN, M. L'emploi actuel de l'écriture latine en Chine. [The present use of Roman script in China.] Bull. Soc.

Linguistique de Paris, 55, no. 1, 1960:xxv-xxvi.
   The new Latinized alphabet is used in parallel with about 3000 simplified Chinese characters.

620
CH'EN, YÜEH. [The problem of the simplification of phonetic characters and the characters used in transliteration.] Chung-kuo yü-wen [Chinese language and writing], 1961:34-37. (In Chinese)

621
HSIAO, MU-HSIEN. [Chinese-English spelling dictionary.] Taipeh, 1962. 100 p. (In Chinese)

622
TIEN, H.C. A guide to the new Latin spelling of Chinese, by H.C. Tien, R. Hsia and P. Penn. Kowloon, Hong Kong, Oriental Book Co., 1962. 64 p. (China reference series, 3)

623
DOUGHERTY, C., S.M. LAMB, and S.E. MARTIN. Chinese character indexes. Berkeley, University of California Press, 1963. 5 v.
   Vol. 2. Romanization index, has a comparative table of five systems: National, Communist, Ošanin (the Russian system, see also 654), Wade-Giles, and Yale.

624
LIBRARY OF CONGRESS. Chinese: Romanization, capitalization and punctuation. Cataloging Service, Bull. 62, Sept. 1963. 8 p.
   Supersedes and augments the instructions published in 1957 and reprinted in 618.

625
OHIO STATE UNIVERSITY. RESEARCH FOUNDATION. Comparative table of Pinyin, Yale, Wade-Giles, Zhuyin Zimu and Gwoyen Romatzyh (tonal spelling) systems. In its Project on linguistic analysis. 1963. p. 37-49.

626
SHARMAN, G. A new Chinese alphabet with graphic tonal spellings. Los Angeles, Monograph Committee, 1963. 14 p.

627
UNITED STATES. ARMY LANGUAGE SCHOOL. Chinese-Mandarin; Wade-Giles romanization drills. Presidio of Monterey, 1963. 21 p.

628
Hanzi Gaige Gailun. [Introduction to the reform of Han characters.] Peking, 1964. 358 p. (In Chinese)
   Comprehensive summary of the reform movement. Displays and explains the simplified Chinese characters introduced by the Communist government. There is a large number of tables comparing many different Latinization and Romanization schemes proposed during the last 150 years.

The Romanized title is given in the form cited, followed on the title page by the Chinese title (here translated). Except for examples of Romanization of single syllables in the tables, and a few examples of foreign surnames and geographical names, the text is in Chinese throughout.

629
KUMAR, B.K. Cataloguing of Chinese books, and problems and prospects of transliteration. <u>Herald of Library Science</u>, <u>5</u>, 1966:86-87.

630
KUMAR, B.K. Filing of entries for Chinese titles. <u>Herald of Library Science</u>, <u>5</u>, 1966:297-300.
   The filing systems used in Taiwan, in the Library of Congress and in the Harvard and Columbia libraries are compared. The first is considered to be cumbersome, the second does not distinguish between different meanings of Romanized syllables, and the third is recommended as best, since it combines Romanization with stroke counts.

631
TING, LEE-HSIA HSU. Problems of cataloging Chinese author and title entries in American Libraries. <u>Library Quarterly</u>, <u>36</u>, no. 1, 1966:1-13.
   A comprehensive survey of Chinese cataloging practices in U.S. libraries. The author concludes that (i) since Romanization does not mean anything to the majority of the catalog users in American libraries, translation of entries should be used wherever possible; (ii) personal names and geographical names should be transcribed according to Wade-Giles; (iii) uniform headings may not be feasible for Chinese material; and (iv) catalogs should serve the readers not the catalogers. The article is a condensation of the author's Master's thesis (University of Texas, 1964).

632
ANDERSON, O.B. Simple and consistent mode of transcription for standard Chinese, Cantonese and Siamese. <u>Libri</u>, <u>17</u>, no. 2, 1967:86-94.
   Proposes a new transcription scheme which is simpler than the Wade-Giles system and expresses the four tones by appended (silent) letters. No diacritical marks are used.

633
LEGEZA, I.L. Guide to transliterated Chinese in the modern Peking dialect. Leiden, Brill, 1968. 2 v.
   Vol. 1. Conversion table of the currently used international and European systems, with comparative tables of initials and finals. - v. 2. Conversion tables of the outdated international and European individual systems with comparative tables of initials and finals. This is the most comprehensive compilation of transcript-

ion systems published to date. There are no less than 50 individual systems, of which 29 are no longer used or have been proposed by individual authors for their own books on Chinese subjects. But 21 systems are actually used in different countries and for different languages, and there is almost no similarity between them, as can be seen from the tables of syllables which show the systems synoptically.

634
ANDERSON, O.B. Konkordans till fyra transkriptionssystem för kinesiskt riksspråk. [Concordance to four transcription systems for standard Chinese.] Lund, Studentlitteratur, 1969. 182 p.

635
ANDERSON, O.B. A concordance to five systems of transcription for standard Chinese. Lund, Studentlitteratur, 1970. 228 p.

636
KAU, PEI ZER. [Simplified Chinese Romanization suitable for typewriting.] Simplified Chinese romanization, available for typewriting. Singapur, 1970. 189 p. (In Chinese, with some explanations in English)
   The title is given first in Chinese (here translated) and then translated into English.

637
ANDERSON, J.D. A comparative study of methods of arranging Chinese author-title catalogs in large American Chinese language collections. New York, Columbia University, 1972. 150 p. (Ph.D. thesis)

638
CH'EN, C.K.H. A standard romanized dictionary of Chinese and Japanese popular surnames. Hanover, N.H., Oriental Society, 1972. 681 p.

***

See also 28, 29, 711.

Transcription of Chinese into individual languages and scripts

Chinese-Devanagari

639
THOMAS, F.W. A Buddhist Chinese text in Brahmi script. Z. Deut. Morgenländ. Ges., 91, 1937:1-48.
   The Brahmi script was used during the 6th and 7th century A.D. and is considered to be an early form of the Devanagari script.

Chinese-Spanish

640
BASOMBRIO, E. Propuesta de solución para las grafías chinas. [Proposal of a solution for Chinese characters.] Revista de

Estudios Clásicos, 10, 1966:133-143.
  Proposes a new transcription system from Chinese into Spanish, and makes comparisons with the Wade-Giles system.

Chinese-French

641
VISSIÈRE, A. Méthode de transcription française des sons chinois, adoptée par le Ministère des Affaires Étrangères. [A method for French transcription of Chinese sounds, adopted by the Ministry of Foreign Affairs.] Bull. Mensuel du Comité de l'Asie Française, 2, no. 12, mars 1912:112-117.

642
DEMIÉVILLE, P. Matériaux pour l'enseignement élémentaire du chinois: écriture, transcription, langue parlée nationale. [Materials for elementary instruction in Chinese: script, transcription, the spoken national language.] Paris, Adrien-Maisonneuve, 1953. 1 v.

Chinese-Romanian

643
CONSTANTIN, G.I. How to transcribe Chinese phonetics into Rumanian. Studia et acta orientalia, 1, 1957:351-353.

644
WECHSLER, B. Transcrierea cuvintelor și numelor chinezești în limba romînă. [Transcription of Chinese words and names into Romanian.] Limba Romînă, 13, 1964:231-244.

Chinese-German

645
LESSING, F., and W. OTHMER. Lehrbuch der nordchinesischen Umgangssprache. [Textbook of the northern Chinese vernacular language.] Tsingtau, 1912.
  The transcription system first proposed in this work has become the standard system used in German-speaking countries.

646
MOSSNER, F. Transliteration chinesischer und japanischer Texte. [Transliteration of Chinese and Japanese texts.] Dokumentation, 7, 1960:149-150.

Chinese-Dutch

647
THYS, E. Enkele tipe voor de transcriptie van Chinese eigennamen. [Some hints for the transliteration of Chinese personal names.] Bibliotheekgids, 27, 1951:71-80.
  A list of authors in Dutch, English and French forms of transcription.

648
MULLIE, J. De Romanizering van de Chinese taal. [The Romanization of the Chinese language.] Brussels, Palais der

Academiën, 1958. (Mededelingen van de Koninklijke Vlaamse Academie voor Wetenschappen, Letteren en Schone Kunsten van België. Klasse der Letteren, 20, no. 5)

Chinese-Polish

649
JABŁOŃSKI, W. Polska transkrypcja pisma chińskiego. [Polish transcription of Chinese script.] Rocznik Orientalistyczny, 10, 1934:87-121.

Chinese-Hungarian

650
LIGETI, L. A kínai irásjegyek magyaros átirása. [Chinese ideograms in Hungarian transcription.] Körösi Csoma Archivium, 1. Kiegészítő kötet, 3. füzet, 1937:249-266.

651
MAGYAR TUDOMÁNYOS AKADÉMIA. A kínai nevek és szavak magyar átirása. [Hungarian transcription of Chinese names and words.] Budapest, 1952.
   A transcription scheme devised by the Hungarian Academy of Sciences for use in Hungarian publications. There are comparative tables for Chinese syllables in Russian, English, French and German transcription.

Cyrillization

652
VASIL'EV, V.P. [A graphic system of Chinese hieroglyphics; a first attempt at a Chinese-Russian dictionary.] Sanktpeterburg, 1867. (In Russian)
   The earliest proposal for a Russian transcription of Chinese.

653
ALEKSEEV, V.M. [The Chinese hieroglyphic script and its Romanization.] Leningrad, Akademija Nauk SSSR, 1932. 178 p.
   This item does not strictly belong here because the system proposed is one of Romanization; however, it is for use of Russian-speaking readers, and is said to have been actually employed until the early 1930'ies. It was called the Sin Wenz (or Latinxua Sin Wenz) system. It was superseded by the Cyrillization scheme of Ošanin (see 654).

654
OŠANIN, I.M. [Chinese-Russian dictionary.] 3rd ed. Moskva, 1959. (In Russian)
   The Cyrillization system used in this dictionary is now the most commonly accepted one in the Soviet Union. The dictionary contains tables of Cyrillization for every Chinese syllable.

655
ALLEN, C.G. Russian transcription of Chinese names. J. Doc., 16, 1960:80-91.
Discusses the differences between the Wade-Giles and the Ošanin system and the resulting difficulties in identifying Chinese names in Russian sources. Tables of comparison between the two systems are given.

656
MACAEV, S.A., and V.G. ORLOV. [Manual for transcription and orthography of Chinese words.] Moskva,"Nauka", 1966. 226 p. (In Russian)

Arabization

657
FORKE, A. Ein islamisches Tractat aus Turkestan. (Chinesisch in arabischer Schrift.) [An Islamic tractate from Turkestan. (Chinese in Arabic script.)] T'oung Pao, 8, 1907:1-76.

658
HASSAN, S.M. Medicinal clay tablets bearing Chinese names in Arabic characters. Islamic Culture, 38, 1964:289-294.
The transcription dates from the 16th century. The names of herbs are transcribed into Arabic.

Chinese-Uigur

659
CSONGOR, B. Ujgúr írásos kínai szórványok. [Chinese in Uigur script.] Budapest, 1947. (Keletázsiai dolgozatok, no. 2)
On transcription of Chinese texts into Uigur. There is an English summary.

Chinese-Korean

660
[Translation of Chinese proverbs into Korean.] Seoul, 1943. 408 p. (In Korean)

661
[Translation of Chinese proverbs into Korean.] Seoul, 1944. 370 p. (In Korean)

Chinese-Tibetan

662
SEDLÁČEK, K. On Tibetan transcription of Chinese characters. Mitt. Inst. Orientforsch. Deut.Akad. Wiss. Berlin, 5, 1957:91-112.

663
SIMON, W. Note on Chinese texts in Tibetan transcription. Bull. Sch. Orient. Afr. Stud., 21, pt.2, 1958:334-343.

664
CHENG, TSAI-FA. [A critical examination of the 'Phags-pa

script transcription of Chinese texts.] In [Festschr. Li Chi], 1967, v.2., p. 933-1003. (In Chinese)
  'Phags-pa (also known as Passepa) is an ancient Tibetan script which was used for the writing of sacred Buddhist texts.

Transcription into Chinese

665
HSIN, HUA. [Handbook of English names, transcribed into Chinese.] Peking, 1965. iv, 381 p. (In Chinese)

Tibetan

Romanization

666
RICHTER, Eberhard. Zum Problem der Schaffung einer einheitlichen Umschrift (Transliteration und Transkription) des Tibetischen. [On the problem of creating a uniform Romanization (transliteration and transcription) of Tibetan.] Z. Deut. Morgenländ. Ges., 114, 1964:171-179.

667
WYLIE, T. Standard system of Tibetan transliteration. Harvard J. of Asiatic Studies, 22, 1959:261-267.

668
LIBRARY OF CONGRESS. Tibetan romanization. Cataloging Service, Bull. 90, Sept. 1970:3-4.

Cyrillization

669
VOROBEVA-DESJATOVSKAJA, M.I. [On the transliteration and transcription of the Tibetan language.] In Voprosy filologij istoričeskij [C], 1961. p. 43-55. (In Russian)

670
SEDLÁČEK, K., and B.V. SEMIČOV. [Again on the transliteration and transcription of Tibetan.] Trudy Akad. Nauk SSSR, Sibirsk. Otd., no. 2, 1965:132-144. (In Russian)
  Has a table of phonetic transcription. The author refers to his earlier article in the same journal, no. 8, 1962 (of which I could not obtain particulars).

***

See also Chinese-Tibetan 662-664. Place names 728.

Thai

Romanization

671
AUROUSSEAU, M. Official Romanization of Thai (Siamese). Geog. J., 98, Sept. 1941:154-155.

672
ROYAL INSTITUTE OF THAILAND. Notification of the Royal Institute concerning the transcription of Thai characters into Roman. J. Thailand Soc., 33, pt. 1, 1941:49-65.

673
UNITED STATES. ARMY. 500th MILITARY INTELLIGENCE GROUP. A guide to the pronunciation of Romanized Burmese. [Tokyo?], 1956. 32 l.

673a
UNITED STATES. ARMY. 500th MILITARY INTELLIGENCE GROUP. A guide to the pronunciation of Romanized Siamese & Lao. [Tokyo?], 1956. 42 l.

674
LIBRARY OF CONGRESS. Romanization - Languages of Burma and Thailand. Cataloging Service, Bull. 76, Oct. 1966. 7 p.
   The table for Thai superseded the one published in Bull. 45, 1958.

675
ANDERSON, O.B. Simple and consistent mode of transcription for standard Chinese, Cantonese, and Siamese. Libri, 17, no. 2, 1967:86-94.
   Proposes a system using only a few diacritical marks and a series of final letters to indicate tones.

Cyrillization

676
PUZICKIJ, E.V. [Some debatable points regarding the Russian transcription of Burmese words.] Narody Azii i Afriki, 1962: 166-169. (In Russian)
   The present Cyrillic transcription of Burmese does not express tonality. The system is modelled on English transcription and thus does not indicate pronunciation for a Russian reader.

677
ZLATOVERHOVA, V.G. [On scientific Russian transcription of Burmese.] Narody Azii i Afriki, 1963:151-156. (In Russian)
   A new proposal for the transcription of vowels, consonants and tones of Burmese into Russian.

Transcription into Thai characters

678
KIN, U THA. Transliteration of foreign names and words into Burmese. J. Burma Research Soc., 22, 1932:35-38.

***

See also Place names 744.

Vietnamese

Romanization

679
AYMONIER, E.F. Nos transcriptions; étude sur les systèmes d'écriture en caractères européens adoptés en Cochinchine française. [Our transcriptions; a study of the writing systems in European characters adopted in French Cochinchina.] Saigon, Imprimerie coloniale, 1886. 63 p.

Cyrillization

680
MHITARIAN, T.T. [Russian transcription of Vietnamese.] Narodi Azii i Afriki, 1962:126-131. (In Russian)
　The present transcription system is incorrect and insufficient. Proposes a better scheme for the Cyrillization of personal names and place names.

Cambodian

681
UNITED STATES. ARMY. 500th MILITARY INTELLIGENCE GROUP. A guide to the pronunciation of Romanized Cambodian. [Tokyo?] 1956. iii, 33 l.

681a
LEWITZ, S. Note sur la translittération du cambodgien. [Note on the transliteration of Cambodian.] Bull. École Française d'Extrême-Orient, 55, 1969:163-169.

IX. LANGUAGES OF NEGRO AFRICA

Romanization

682
TUCKER, A.N. African alphabets and the telegraph problem. Bantu Studies, 10, 1936:67-75.

683
LA VERGNE DE TRESSAN, DU Pour une transcription phonétique peule unifiée. [For a uniform phonetic transcription of Fula.] Bull. Inst. Français Afr. Noire, 13, 1951:916-923.
　Fula is now written in Arabic script. A Romanization scheme is proposed, and examples of text in Arabic and Romanized script are given.

684
JACQUOT, A. L'orthographe française et la transcription des langues vernaculaires. [French orthography and the transcription of vernacular languages.] Brazzaville, Conseil consultatif de recherches de l'I.E.C., 1956. 7 p.
　On the phonetic transcription of African languages lacking a script.

685
MONTEIL, V. Sur la transcription des langues africaines.

[On the transcription of African languages.] <u>Bull. de l'Institut Français d'Afrique Noir</u>, <u>28</u>, no. 3-4, 1966:723-730.
  On the transcription of Sudano-Guinean languages.

686
GALAND, L. Une réunion d'experts pour l'alphabetisation de certaines langues africaines. [A meeting of experts on the alphabetization of certain African languages.] <u>Compte rendu du Groupe Linguistique d'Études Chamito-Semitiques</u>, <u>11</u>, 1967: 1.
  Alphabets for ten West and Central African languages are
  proposed.

687
BRAUNER, S. Bisherige Ergebnisse bei der Schaffung von Transkriptionssystemen für die nationalen Sprachen der Republik Mali. [Results so far achieved in the creation of transcription systems for the national languages of the Republic of Mali.] <u>Mitt. Inst. Orientforsch., Deut. Akad. Wiss. Berlin</u>, <u>14</u>, 1968:375-385.

Arabization

688
MULLER, P.J. Afrikaanse geskrifte in arabiese karakters. [African scripts in Arabic characters.] <u>Quart. Bull. S. Afr. Libr.</u>, <u>15</u>, 1960:36-45.

X.   AMERICAN LANGUAGES

689
BERENDT, K.H. Analytical alphabet for the Mexican & Central American languages. New York, American Church Press Co., 1869. 14 p.
  A scheme for the transcription of the Maya language. As
  an example, the Lord's Prayer is given in Maya, Spanish
  and German, using the author's scheme.

XI.   GYPSY LANGUAGES

690
KOCHANOWSKI, J. Transcription de la langue tsigane. [Transcription of the Gypsy language.] <u>Études Tsiganes</u>, <u>11</u>, no. 1, 1965:3-12; no. 3:13-17.

***

XII. TRANSLITERATION AND TRANSCRIPTION OF PLACE NAMES

Romanization

(a) General

691
HERSCHEL, Sir J.F.W. Transcription of place-names and unwritten languages. In his Essays from the Edinburgh and Quarterly Reviews, with addresses and other pieces. London, Longmans, 1857. p. 745-750.
   This was first published as Appendix to the author's "Admiralty Manual of Scientific Engineering" in 1848.

692
GREAT BRITAIN. WAR OFFICE. INTELLIGENCE DIVISION. The following system of orthography for native names of places adopted by the Council of the Royal Geographical Society, the Foreign and Colonial Offices, Admiralty and War Office is to be adhered to in all Intelligence Division publications. London, 1892. 1 p.

693
CHISHOLM, G.G. Some points connected with the orthography of place-names. In International Geographical Congress. 6th, 1895. Report. p. 483-492.

694
PUSSIÉ, E. Unification internationale de translitération en caractères latins pour la transcription des noms géographiques. [International unification of transliteration into Roman characters for the transcription of geographical names.] In International Geographical Congress. 6th, 1895. Report. p. 513-516.

695
RICCHIERI, G. Per la trascrizione e la pronuncia dei nomi geografici. [On the transcription and pronunciation of geographical names.] In International Geographical Congress. 6th, 1895. Report. p. 505-512.
   This was reprinted by the Istituto italiano d'arti grafiche (Bergamo, 1927).

696
GARNIER, C. T.R.G. Méthode de transcription rationelle générale des noms géographiques s'appliquant à toutes les écritures usitées dans le monde ... [T.R.G. Method of general rational transcription of geographical names, applicable to all scripts used in the world...] Paris, Leroux, 1899.
   This was the work of a brilliant young linguist and geographer who died before the work was published. Although based on the needs of French users, it contains much of value for general use, and is still considered to be one of the basic contributions to the subject.

697
SCHRADER, F. La Méthode de transcription rationelle générale des noms géographiques par Christian Garnier. <u>In</u> International Geographical Congress. 7th, 1899. <u>Verhandlungen.</u> p. 974-981.
   A critical appraisal of 696.

698
KNOX, A. Rules for the transliteration of place-names occurring on foreign maps. London, War Office, 1906. iii, 83 p.

699
EZERSKIJ, T.V. L'alphabet universel, transcription des noms géographiques de tous les pays. [The universal alphabet, transcription of geographical names of all countries.] Rome, 1912. 25 p.
   A report submitted to the 10th International Geographical Congress, 1912.

699a
EZERSKIJ, T.V. Универсалный географический алфавить. Alphabet géographique universel. Alfabeto geografico universale. Geographical universal alphabet. Universales geographisches Alphabet. Geografiskt universal alfabet. St. Petersbourg, 1913.

700
CLIFFORD, E.H.M. Recording native place names. <u>Geogr. J.</u>, <u>109</u>, 1947:99-102.
   Recommends the RGS II system for general use.

701
GAVIRA, J. La cuestión de las transcripciones geográficas. [The question of geographical transcription.] <u>Estudios Geográficos</u>, <u>10</u>, 1949:403-444.

702
TÄUBER, H. Ueber eine Konferenz zu Fragen der Transkription geographischer Namen. [On a conference devoted to questions of transcription of geographical names.] <u>Petermanns geographische Mitt.</u>, <u>100</u>, 1956:81-84.
   On a conference held by the Soviet Geographical Society in Leningrad, 1955. See also 730.

703
TÄUBER, H. Die Lösung des Transkriptionsproblems. [The solution of the transcription problem.] <u>Petermanns geographische Mitt.</u>, <u>101</u>, 1957:314-315.
   On the transcription of Russian place names into German, using the Soviet standard (which later became practically the ISO standard), instead of phonetic transcription.

704
UUSTALU, E. Double transliteration of geographical names. <u>Amer. Slavic and East European Review</u>, <u>15</u>, 1956:244-247.

705
AUROUSSEAU, M. The rendering of geographical names. London, Hutchinson, 1957. 148 p.
   See also 44.

706
UNITED NATIONS CONFERENCE ON THE STANDARDIZATION OF GEOGRAPHICAL NAMES. [1st] Geneva, 1967.

707
BARSAN, A., and S. DRAGOMIRESCU. Principes utilisès dans la graphie des noms géographiques étrangers et les solutions adoptées en Roumanie dans ce domaine. [Principles used in the writing of foreign geographical names, and the solution adopted in Romania.] Rév. Roumaine Géol., 13, no. 2, 1969: 185-189.

708
GRUCZA, F. Probleme der Transposition von fremden Ortsnamen. (Zu einer Methode der Lautrekonstruktion.) [Problems of transposition of foreign place names. (On a method of sound reconstruction.).] Biuletyn Fonograficzny, 9, 1968:105-120.

709
PUSTKOWSKI, R. Die Schreibweise geographischer Namen in deutschsprachigen Karten. [The spelling of geographical names on German language maps.] Vermessungstechnik, 16, no. 9, 1968:337-338, 351.
   On the work of two committees in East and West Germany.

710
UNITED NATIONS CONFERENCE ON THE STANDARDIZATION OF GEOGRAPHICAL NAMES. 2nd. London, 1972.
   The following papers dealt with matters of transcription and transliteration: Writing systems; transfer of names from one writing system into another. Report of the Working Group on a single romanization system (Part 1). (E/CONF.61/L.5) - Writing systems. (E/CONF.61/L21). - Transcription of geographical names in the Republic of Viet-Nam. (E/CONF.61/L.10).

711
UNITED STATES. DEPT. OF STATE. OFFICE OF THE GEOGRAPHER. Romanization guide. Washington, D.C., 1972. 92 p.
   Issued jointly with the U.S. Board on Geographic Names, and based on its system. The following languages are covered: Amharic, Arabic, Bulgarian, Burmese, Chinese, Faeroese, Greek, Hebrew, Icelandic, Japanese, Khmer, Korean, Laotian, Lappish, Maldivian, Mongolian, Nepali, Pashtu, Persian, Russian, Serbian and Macedonian, Thai, Ukrainian. For each language, there is a table of Romanization and introductory notes on special problems. The book is issued from time to time with revisions.

Romanization

(b) By source language or script

712
HUNTER, Sir W.W. Guide to the orthography of Indian proper names, with a list showing the true spelling for all post towns and villages in India. Calcutta, 1871. xiii, 146 p.

713
HUNTER, Sir W.W. The Imperial gazetteer of India ... 2nd ed. London, Trübner, 1885-87. 14 v.
  "Notes on transliteration" in vol. 1, mainly based on the scheme proposed by Sir William Jones (see 391).

714
Transliteration of place names from modern Greek. Geogr. J., 97, 1941:156-157.

715
UNITED STATES. BOARD ON GEOGRAPHICAL NAMES. Transliteration system for Persian geographical names; the BGN/PCGN system. Washington, 1960. 5 p.
  Supersedes an earlier version (see 721).

716
ROYAL GEOGRAPHICAL SOCIETY OF LONDON. The R.G.S. II system for the transliteration of Russian and the treatment of conventional names. London, 1938. 4 p.
  Reprinted from the Geogr. J., 92, 1938:446-449, where the article is signed E.D.R., M.A.

717
KOSACK, H.P. Die neue amtliche Lateinschrift und die Entwicklung des Transkriptionsproblems von den ältesten Karten Russlands bis auf die heutige Zeit. [The new official Roman script and the development of the transcription problem from the oldest maps of Russia until the present time.] Nachrichten aus dem Reichsvermessungsdienst, 1943:193-209.

718
GELLERT, J.F. Zur Transkription geographischer Namen und Bezeichnungen aus der kyrillischen Schrift ins Deutsche. [On the transcription of geographical names and designations from Cyrillic script into German.] Petermanns geographische Mitt., 93, 1949:78-80.

719
GELLERT, J.F. Richtlinien zur einheitlichen Wiedergabe der geographischen Namen und Bezeichnungen aus der Sowjetunion im deutschen Schrifttum. [Guidelines for the uniform rendering of geographical names and designations from the Soviet Union in the German literature.] Petermanns geographische Mitt., 94, 1950:38-40.

720
PETZSCHNER, H. Zur Uebertragung von geographischen Bezeichnungen und Lagerstättennamen aus dem Russischen ins Deutsche.

[On the Romanization of geographical designations and names of mineral deposits from Russian into German.] <u>Bergakademie</u>, <u>14</u>, 1962:104-107.

721
UNITED STATES. BOARD ON GEOGRAPHIC NAMES. The transliteration of Arabic and Persian ... Washington, D.C., 1946. 9 p.

722
UNITED STATES. BOARD ON GEOGRAPHIC NAMES. Transliteration system for Arabic geographic names; the BGN/PCGN system. Washington, D.C., 1957. 5 p.

723
McCUNE, S. Romanization of place names in Korea. <u>Geogr. Rev.</u>, <u>31</u>, 1941:150-152.
   Recommends the McCune-Reischauer system for Korean place names instead of Romanized Japanese.

724
SENAVERATNA, J.M. Transliteration of Ceylon place-names. <u>Ceylon Literary Register</u>, ser. 3, 1935/36:19-25.

725
UNITED STATES. ARMY MAP SERVICE. GEOGRAPHIC NAMES BOARD. Guide to special readings of Chinese characters, for the use of place-name romanizers. Washington, D.C., [194-?] 21 l.

726
Romanization of Chinese place-names. <u>Geogr. J.</u>, <u>102</u>, 1943: 67-71.

727
GELLERT, J.F. Die Wiedergabe der chinesischen geographischen Namen und Bezeichnungen in lateinischer Buchstabenschrift. [The rendering of Chinese geographical names and designations in Roman characters.] <u>Forschungen und Fortschritte</u>, <u>38</u>, 1964:12-16.

728
BAILEY, F.M. Spelling of Tibetan place names. <u>Geogr. J.</u>, <u>97</u>, 1941:120-122.

Cyrillization

(a) General

729
TJURIN, S.A. [Some principles of rendering geographical names on maps.] <u>Izv. Akad. Nauk SSSR., Ser. Geogr.</u>, 1953: 89-94. (In Russian)

730
[Conference on the transcription of geographical names.] <u>Izv. Vses. Geogr. Obšč.</u>, 1955:387-405. (In Russian)
   See also 702.

731
REFORMATSKIJ, A.A. [On the supply and transformation of geographical names on Russian maps.] In Transkripcija geografičeskih nazvanij [C], 1960. (In Russian)

732
SUPERANSKAJA, A.V. [Questions regarding the orthography of geographical names.] In Transkripcija geografičeskih nazvanij [C], 1960. (In Russian)

733
Transkripcija geografičeskih nazvanij. [Transcription of geographical names.] Edited by E.M. Murzaev. Moskva, 1960. 1 v. (In Russian)
   A collection of articles on the subject.

734
BERG, S.L. [On the combinations of sounds and letters in transcribed names which are inappropriate to Russian.] In Orfografia sobstvennih imen [C], 1964. p.104-116. (In Russ.)

735
BONDARUK, G.P., and S.A. TJURIN. [The orthography of geographical names.] In Orfografia sobstvennih imen [C], 1964. p. 11-20. (In Russian)

736
BROCKI, Z. Wkład polskich uczonych w ustalenie rosyjskiej transkrypcji nazw geograficznych. [Scientific Polish contribution to the determination of Russian transcriptions of geographical names.] Czasopismo geograficzne, 37, 1966:325.

737
UNION OF SOVIET SOCIALIST REPUBLICS. MINISTERSTVO VNUTRENNIH DEL. [Instruction for the rendering of geographical names on maps.] Moskva, 1952-66. 1 v. (In Russian)
   The official guidelines of the Soviet Ministry of Interior Affairs.

Cyrillization

(b) By source language or script

738
SAVINA, V.I. [Dictionary of Russian transcription for Iranian geographical names.] Moskva, 1961. 215 p. (In Russian)

739
GOLUBEV, Z.D. [On the rendering of taxonomic terms which form part of German geographical names.] In Toponomastika i transkripcija [C], 1964. (In Russian)

740
KUZNECOVA, V.I., and NIKOLAEVA, N.V. [Some points concerning the rendering of English place names in Russian on maps and atlases.] Vest. Leningr. Univ., Ser. Biol., 13, 1958: 143-151. (In Russian)

741
SUPERANSKAJA, A.V. [On the question of practical transcription of English names of countries.] In Toponomastika i transkripcija [C], 1964. (In Russian)

741a
Toponomastika i transkripcija. [The study of place names and transcription.] Edited by S.G. Barhudarov et al. Moskva, "Nauka", 1964. 199 p. (In Russian)
   A collection of articles on problems in the transcription of place names and proper names.

742
UNION OF SOVIET SOCIALIST REPUBLICS. CENTRAL'NIJ NAUČNO-ISSLEDOVATEL'SKII INSTITUT GEODEZII, AEROSEMKI I KARTOGRAFII. OTDELENIE TRANSKRIPCII. [Instructions on the rendering of place names in Arabic countries on maps.] Moskva, "Nauka", 1966. 1 v. (In Russian)
   The official guidelines of the Central Scientific Research Institute for Geodesy, Aerial Surveys and Cartography.

743
PETRUŠEVSKIJ, B.A. [On the question of the transcription of local geographical names in Central Asia and Kazakhstan.] Izv. vses. geogr. obšč., 1958:185-186. (In Russian)

744
EPŠTEJN, V.G. [Rules for the transcription of Burmese place names into Russian.] Moskva, Izd. Vostočnoj Lit., 1959. 54 p. (In Russian)

Transcription into Chinese

745
HSIN, HUA. [Handbook of English names, transcribed into Chinese.] Peking, 1965. iv, 381 p. (In Chinese)
   Contains transcriptions of English personal names and place names into Chinese characters.

***

ADDENDA

The following entries are numbered in the sequence in which they should appear in the main part of the bibliography, e.g. 182a comes between 182 and 183. All addenda entries have been indexed.

182a
ROMANO, D. Un texto en aljamía hebraicoárabe. [A text in Hebrew-Arabic script.] Sefarad, 29, 1969:313-318.

183a
CAHEN, C. La leçon de quelques transcriptions arabes de noms français médiévaux. [What to learn from some Arabic transcriptions of Medieval French names.] Romania, 91, 1970:416-418.

239a
PORTUGAL. INSPECÇÃO GERAL DOS PRODUCTOS AGRICOLAS E INDUSTRIAS. REPARTIÇÃO DE NORMALIZAÇÃO. Sistema internacional para a transliteração does caracteres cirílicos. [International system of transliteration for Cyrillic characters.] Lisboa, 1961. (NP-47)
    The official Portuguese transliteration standard for Cyrillic, identical with ISO/R9.

240a
INSTITUT BELGE DE NORMALIZATION. Système international pour la translitération. Caractères cyrilliques. [International system for transliteration. Cyrillic characters.] Bruxelles, 1957. (NBN 447/1957)
    The official Belgian transliteration standard for Cyrillic, identical with ISO/R9.

242a
ROMANIA. OFFICIUL DE STAT PENTRU STANDARDE. Transliterația caracterelor chirilice sistem ISO. [Transliteration of Cyrillic characters according to the ISO system.] București, 1956. (STAS R 5309)
    The standard conforms to ISO/R9 but is used only for international purposes; for domestic use, the rules of the Academiei Republicii Socialiste România for Russian, Bulgarian and Greek characters are mandatory.

257a
DENMARK. DANSK STANDARDISERINGSRÅD. Translitteration af kyrilliske bogstaver. [Transliteration of Cyrillic characters.] København, 1953. (DS 378)
    The official Danish transliteration standard for Cyrillic, conforming to ISO/R9, except for one character. There is a separate standard for the transliteration of modern

Russian with an appendix on the transliteration of
Russian names (see 361a).

267a
HUNGARY. SZABVÁNYÜGYI HIVATAL. Cirilbetűs címek átírása
könyvtári és dokumentációs célokra. [Transliteration of
entries in Cyrillic characters.] Budapest, 1955. (MSZ 3394)
   The official Hungarian transliteration standard for Cyrillic, following ISO/R9 with adaptations to the Hungarian
   alphabet.

273 a
BULGARIA. INSTITUT PO STANDARTIZACJA, MERKI I IZMERITELNI
UREDI. [Transliteration of Bulgarian characters into Roman
characters.] Sofia, 1956. (BDS 1596-56)
   The official Bulgarian transliteration standard, follow-
   ing ISO/R9.

278a
MUFTIĆ. T. [On the orthography of Arabic script used for
Serbo-Croatian.] Prilozi za Orijentalnu Filologiju i Isto-
riju, no. 14-15, 1964-65:101-121. (In Serbian)

278b
LEHFELDT, W. Ein Beitrag zur Erforschung des serbo-kroati-
schen Aljamiado-Schrifttums. [A contribution to the study
of Serbo-Croatian Aljamiado literature.] Südostforschungen,
28, 1969:94-122.

289a
REYCHMAN, J. Nowe prace o zalytkach piśmennictwa polsko-
białoruskiego pismem arabskiw. [New studies on Polish-
Whiterussian texts in Arabic script.] Przegląd Orientalistyczny, 4, 1970:344-353.

316a
U.S.S.R. KOMITET STANDARTOV, MER I IZMERITEL'NYH PRIBOROV.
[Transliteration of Russian terms into Roman characters.]
Moskva, 1957. (OST/VKS 8483)
   The official Soviet standard for the transliteration of
   Cyrillic characters as used in Russian into Roman char-
   acters. Identical with ISO/R9. An earlier version of
   this standard, published in 1935, followed the rules of
   the British Museum, with certain exceptions.

329a
SYSTEM DEVELOPMENT CORPORATION. Instruction in transliterating Russian into English. Santa Monica, Calif., 1969.
37 p.
   A programmed instruction course for library technicians,
   purportedly not requiring a knowledge of Russian.

361a
DENMARK. DANSK STANDARDISERINGSRÅD. Translitteration af det moderne russiske alfabet. [Transliteration of the modern Russian alphabet.] København, 1964. (DS 378.1)
   A supplement to the official Danish transliteration standard for Cyrillic characters (see item 257a), with an appendix:

Bilagsblad A. Eksempler på translitteration af russiske navner. [Appendix A. Examples of transliteration of Russian names.]

441a
AMERICAN NATIONAL STANDARDS INSTITUTE. Proposed standard Romanization of Hebrew. Cincinnati, Ohio, 1972. 16 l.
   At the time of the compilation of this bibliography the standard had not yet been officially approved but existed only in draft form. It is included here because it is expected that it will be approved essentially in the form of this draft. The standard provides for four different Romanization schemes: (i) General purpose Romanization; (ii) More exact Romanization; (iii) Narrow transliteration; and (iv) Computer-compatible transliteration.

450a
ACADEMY OF THE HEBREW LANGUAGE. [Transcription from foreign languages into Hebrew.] Zikhronot ha-aqademya, 17, 5730 [1970]: 25-32; 66-77; 83-94; 97-120.

   The report of a subcommittee which studied the issue, discussion on it, and the final decision of the Academy on the rendering of sounds in foreign names and words in Hebrew characters. The scheme has not yet been published in tabular form.

561a
AMERICAN NATIONAL STANDARDS INSTITUTE. System for the Romanization of Japanese. New York, 1972. (ANSI Z.39.11-1972)
   Essentially the same as the LC scheme, except that the phonetic change of n to m before certain letters is ignored. Writings in classical Chinese by Japanese authors as well as other works in classical Chinese where the text incorporates Japanese "reading marks" (kunten) are covered, as well as material in which Japanese words or sentences are an integral part of a bibliographical unit.

561b
BRITISH STANDARDS INSTITUTION. Romanization of Japanese. London, 1972. (B.S. 4812:1972)
   Follows essentially the Hepburn system, with notes on modifications, some information on other systems, and a list of variants.

AUTHOR AND TITLE INDEX

Numbers refer to items. All names are filed as spelled, disregarding any diacritical marks. Titles of nobility have been omitted from personal names. Titles of works lacking an author attribution (anonyma, collective works, etc.) are listed, except for Chinese and Japanese titles. Anonymous articles in periodicals have not been listed.

A., M. 716
Abdul Huq, A.M. 127
Academy of the Hebrew Language 432, 450a
L'Adoption des charactères latins en Turquie en 1928 507
Alekseev, V.M. 653
Allen, C.G. 227, 655
Aman, M.M. 482
Amburger, E. 371
American Library Association 65, 86, 90, 529, 554, 618
American National Standards Institute 441a, 486, 561a
Anderson, J.D. 637
Anderson, O.B. 632, 634, 635, 675
Andreev, V.D. 274
Andrejčin, L. 362, 366, 369
Asmous, F.C. 307
Associação Brasileira de Normas Técnicas 239
Association Française de Normalisation 241, 437, 477
Aston, W.G. 527
Aurousseau, M. 44, 219, 671, 705
Avanesov, R.I. 47
Aymonier, E.F. 679
Axon, E. 534

B., C. 305
Baba, S. 561
Bachmaier, A. 16, 17, 18
Bacon, R. 156, 423
Bailey, F.M. 728
Bargès, J.J.L. 425
Barhudarov, S.G. 387, 741a
Barndt, G. 247
Barnett, K.M.A. 607
Bărsan, A. 707
Baskakov, N.A. 521
Basombrio, E. 640
Basset, E. 308
Batakliev, G. 171
Battelle Memorial Institute 321
Bayerl, B. 352
Beetle, B. 90
Ben Yehuda, M. 450
Ben Zvi, Y. 448

Berendt, K.H. 689
Berg, S.L. 734
Berkov, V.P. 374
Bertram, G. 443
Biblioteca Apostolica Vaticana 89, 187
Bidwell, C.E. 234
Birnbaum, E. 514
Birnbaum, S.A. 196, 196a, 197, 198
Blake, R.P. 172
Blanken, R.R. 80
Bolland, W. 502
Bolton, H.C. 295a
Bombaci, A. 511
Bondaruk, G.P. 735
Boodberg, P.A. 601
Bosch Vilá, J. 182
Bourgeois, H. 183, 278
Braun, F. 291
Braun, H. 148, 492, 513
Braune, G. 249
Brauner, S. 687
British Academy 143, 205, 457
British Standards Institution 160, 226, 483, 561b
British Museum 88, 186
Brockelmann, C. 462
Brocki, Z. 264, 736
Brown, R.G. 408
Brugmann, K. 108
Bruhn, P. 347, 355
Brutis, P. de 423a, 512
Brux, A.A. 429, 459
Buchanan, R.E. 158
Bulgaria. Institut po Standartizacja, Merki i Izmeritelni Uredi 273a
Burgess, J. 402
Bushell, H.S. 221
Busquets Mulet, J. 181

C., D. 456
Cahen, C. 183a
Caillemer, A. 490
Carr, D. 544, 547
Castagné, J.A. 516, 517
Catford, J.C. 59
Center for Applied Linguistics 77
Československé Tiskové Kanceláře 414a
Charen, T. 330
Chatterji, S.K. 101, 112, 116
Ch'en, C.K.H. 562, 638
Ch'en, Ch'ing-Chin 553
Ch'en, Yüeh 620
Cheng, Tsai-Fa 664

Chi, T'ieh-Hen   585
Chiang, Ching-Fu   591
Chisholm, G.G.   693
Choo, Chang Soh   82
Choroszuszyna, J.   265
Chou, Pien-Ming   599
Cirot, G.   178
Clifford, E.H.M.   700
Commission Internationale de Coopération Intellectuelle   42
Cohen, M.   619
Conference of University Teachers of Russian   304
Constantin, G.I.   643
Corta, J.F.   596
Costa, T.   173
Crane, E.J.   305a
Crome, H.   326, 352
Csongor, B.   659
Cutter, C.A.   85

Damiani, E.   208, 209, 210-212
Danelia, S.   499
Danişman, N.   463
De Francis, J.   597, 605
Demiéville, P.   642
Denmark. Dansk Standardiseringsråd   257a, 361a
Deutscher Normenausschuss   253
Dezsö, L.   268, 271, 275, 368
Dick, G.   343
Diehl, E.   335
Diringer, D.   63
Ditten, H.   164a, 169
Dobrianskij, S.   233
Dolgopol'skij, A.B.   189
Doroszewski, W.   56
Dougherty, C.   623
Dragomirescu, S.   707
Duden   350
Dunlap, K.   307
Duridanov, I.   203
Duyvendak, J.J.L.   609

Edelmann, R.   435
Edmonds, C.J.   139
Educational Association of China   580
Eichhoff, F.G.   4, 6
El-Hadi, M.M., see el-Hadi, M.M.
Elahi, F.   413
Ellis, A.J.   7, 11
Elsner, H.A.   248
Emerton, J.A.   444

Encyclopedia Judaica 442
Engelbach, R. 496
Epštejn, V.G. 744
Erasmus 157
Ezerskij, T.V. 699

Fabergé, A.C. 318
Fahmi, A.A. 468
Felix, J. 280
Fennah, R.G. 159
Fernandez-Galiano, M. 167, 168, 331
Filipova-Bajrova, M. 170
Fischer, K.A. 501
Foord, E. 302
Forchhammer, J. 39
Forke, A. 657
Foulché-Delbosc, R. 177
Foy, K. 509
France. Armée 489
Franklin, D. 325
Fritschy, G.J.M. 217, 349
Frontard, R. 54
Fukuda, N. 545
Furfey, P.M. 307

Gakovich, R. 235
Galand, L. 686
Gardner, C.S. 588
Garnier, C. 696
Garthwaite, L. 109
Gavira, J. 701
Geitler, L. 155
Gellert, J.F. 718, 719, 727
Georgievits, B. 510
Germany. Bundesdruckerei 64
Gerych, G. 320
Gessner, C. 424
Giles, H.A. 578
Giljarevskij, R.S. 229, 315, 379, 386, 388
Gleichen, E. 35, 44, 458
Goldman, E.A. 421
Golubev, Z.D. 739
Gorekar, N.S. 124
Gramenz, F.T. 201a
Great Britain. War Office 297, 692
Gregory, J.W. 300
Grivnin, K.S. 379
Grucza, F. 708
Guggenheim-Grünberg, F. 193, 195
Gvozdev, A.N. 50

H., A.R.   456
el-Hadi, M.M.   479
Hälsig, M.   129
Hamilton, C.H.   102
Hamp, E.P.   318
Han'gui, H.   532
<u>Hanzi Gaige Gailun</u>   628
Harkness, H.   104
Harrington, J.P.   309
Hassan, S.M., <u>see</u> Mahdihassan, S.
Hatsukade, I.   539
Häusler, F.   356
Haykin, D.J.   340
Hazai, G.   515
Heffening, W.   510
Henkel, R.   565
Henze, P.G.   28
Hermelink, H.   476
Hermenau, O.   338
Herschel, J.F.W.   691
Hickman, J.B.   310
Hiromatsu, H.   560
Hirth, F.   581
Hochstein, I.   254
Hofbibliothek. Vienna   84
Hope, E.R.   608
Horiuchi, Y.   555, 555a
Horodyski, B.   260
Hrdlička, A.   307
Hřivnáč, J.   285
Hsia, R.   622
Hsia, Tao-Tai   614
Hsiao, Mu-Hsien   621
Hsin, Hua   202, 665, 745
Huart, C.   488
Hungary. Szabványügyi hivatal   267a
Hunter, W.W.   712, 713
Hus, J.   32
Hüsing, G.   407

ISO, <u>see</u> International Organization for Standardization
Iivainen, L.   200
Imart, G.   518
India. Ministry of Education   117
Ineichen, G.   491
Institut Belge de Normalisation   240a
<u>Instruktionen für die alphabetischen Kataloge</u>   87
International Atomic Energy Agency   237
International Congress of Orientalists   403, 404, 581
International Organization for Standardization   58, 165, 222, 236, 238, 434, 436, 475

Israel. Ministry of Interior. Minorities Dept. 494
Ivancev, S. 282, 287

Jabłoński, W. 649
Jabotinsky, Z. 431
Jackson, A.V.W. 141
Jacquot, A. 684
Jahr, W. 332
Jakobson, R.O. 324
Jakubowski, W. 364
<u>Jewish Encyclopedia</u> 426
Jimbo, K. 540
Jóna, E. 363
Jones, D. 114, 132, 549
Jones, M.B. 214
Jones, W. 391
Jopson, N.B. 293
<u>Jüdisches Lexikon</u> 427
Jušmanov, N.V. 370
Južbasev, N. 503

Kafafi, M. 472
Kahla, M. 365
Kalakuckaja, L.P. 380
Kalan, P. 74
Kančev, I. 530
Karlgren, B. 582
Karum, L.S. 313
Kau, Pei Zer 636
Kempf, Z. 415
Kennedy, E.S. 476
Kent, F.L. 49
Kerner, R.J. 206
Khera, K.L. 121
Kibrik, A.E. 500
Kin, U Tha 678
Kiparsky, V. 201a, 375
Kisinas, I. 445
Kjellberg, L. 258, 259
Klimaszewska, K. 262, 263, 265
Kniesza, I. 267
Knowles, J. 109, 110, 111, 111a
Knox, A. 698
Kochanowski, J. 690
Kodzasov, S.V. 500
Koljada, G.I. 381
Kononov, A.N. 508
Koopmans, J. 420
Kosack, H.P. 717
Koschmider, E. 243
Kosolapoff, G.M. 310

Kotlaba, F. 232
Kral, W. 223, 341, 342
Kretschmar, F. 343
Kristoforid, K. 154
Krylova, N.V. 229
Kuei, Chung-Shu 612
Kuhn, E.W.A. 66
Kumar, B.K. 629, 630
Kuznecova, V.I. 201, 740
Kwei, see Kuei, Chung-Shu

Ladefroux, M. 478
Lamb, S.M. 623
Langlès, L.M. 393, 525
Lauch, A. 357
La Vergne de Tressan, D. 683
Lazard, G. 145
Lazarek, W. 57
Leaman, C. 579
Leclercq, H. 163
Legeza, I.L. 633
Lehfeldt, W. 278b
Leont'ev, A.A. 378
Lepsius, K.R. 9, 14, 452
Leskien, A. 272
Leslie, D. 449
Lessing, F. 645
Leva, A.E. 136
Lévi, I. 455
Lewis, K. 77
Lewitz, S. 681a
Library of Congress 100, 120, 125, 126, 128, 130, 131, 133, 134, 135,
    138, 147, 149, 150, 166, 484, 497, 569, 570, 573, 574, 624, 668, 674
Ligeti, L. 524, 650
Lin, T'ao 606
Lodwick, F. 3
Löhr, H. 96, 566
London, I.D. and M.B. 318
Lotz, J. 33
Lu, Chin 600
Luc Kynh, see Lu, Chin
Lyon, H.T. 454

Macaev, S.A. 656
Mach, O. 245
Machado, J.P. 487
MacKenzie, D.N. 142
Magyar Tudományos Akadémia 651
Mahdihassan, S. 123, 450, 658
Maimon, Z. 73
Maksimova, L.K. 382

Malzac, A.G. 469
Mamiya, F. 542
Mangold, M. 60, 61
Marsden, W. 395, 396
Martin, S.E. 623
Matsumura, T. 558
Matthews, W.K. 218
Mattice, H.A. 543
Matušík, A. 5
McCune, G.M. 528
McCune, S. 723
Megrelidze, I.V. 493
Mehta, J.C. 81
Meinhof, K. 37
Mel'nikov, E.P. 283
Meuvret, C. 75
Meyriat, J. 52
Mhitarian, T.T. 680
Mieli, A. 461, 464
Millás-Vallicrosa, J.M. 179, 181
Minissi, N. 55
Minorsky, V.F. 140
Mirowicz, A. 364
Mish, J.L. 552
Miyazaki, S. 559
Moid, A. 137
Molnár, N. 152, 269, 498
Monier-Williams, M. 97, 105, 107
Montagu-Nathan, M. 303
Monteil, V. 685
Morison, W.A. 294, 314
Morris, H. 21
Mossner, F. 646
Muftic, T. 278a
Mühlpfordt, G. 344
Mulisch, H. 190
Muljačić, Z. 276
Müller, F. 34
Müller, F.M. 10
Muller, P.J. 688
Mullie, J. 648
Murzaev, E.M. 733
Musaev, K.M. 30

Nagy, E. 520
Nationalbibliothek. Vienna, see Hofbibliothek. Vienna
Nedkov, B. 493
Neiswender, R. 320
Newman, F.W. 451
Ni, Hai-Shu 603, 604
Nichols, D.G. 307
Nicolas, L. 455

Nikolaeva, N.V. 740
<u>Novum instrumentum omne</u> 157
Nougayrol, J. 26
Nowicki, P. 446

Ogura, S. 531
Ohio State University Research Foundation 625
Olesch, R. 336
Oliverius, Z.F. 284
Oppenheimer, H. 439
<u>Orfografija sobstvennyh imen</u> 383
Orlov, V.G. 656
Orne, J. 322, 323
Ošanin, I.M. 654
Osborn, A. 87
Osterman, G.F. von 46
Othmer, W. 645

Paclt, J. 220, 225
Pahov, P. 174
Palestine 428, 460
Palmer, F.M. 311
Palmer, H.E. 537
Paper, H.H. 194
Paréja, F.M. 471a, 473
Parsell, J.R. 24, 25, 27
Patil, G.M. 122
Paulausks, J. 204
Pavek, W.J. 23
Paxton, E.H. 467
Peiser, F.E. 406
Penn, P. 622
Petruševkij, B.A. 743
Petzschner, H. 720
<u>Phonetic transcription and transliteration</u> 36, 37, 38
Pierson, J.L. 536
Piette, J.R.F. 76
Pirug, L. 289
Po Chia Hsing 613
Podborny, J.G. 95, 228
Polski Komitet Normalizacyjny 261
Poppe, N. 523
Portugal. Inspecção Geral dos Productos Agricolas e Industrias. Repartição de Normalização 239a
Poulain, J. 433, 436
Poussié, E. 694
Pouzar, Z. 232
Preisigke, F. 419
Pring, J.T. 162
Pring, S.W. 300
Pulleyblanck, E.G. 103

Pustkowski, R. 709
Puzickij, E.V. 676

R., E.D. 716
Raab, H. 353, 358, 359
Rabenstein, B.H. 79
Radó, G. 270
Rajagopalachari, C. 571
Ranganathan, S.R. 71, 93, 411
Rather, L.J. 31
Ray, D.T. 318
Ray, P.S. 118
Razran, G. 317, 318
Reck, H.F. 250, 252, 348
Redhouse, T.W. 453
Reformatskij, A.A. 319, 376, 383, 731
<u>Regeln zur Transkription von russischen Eigen- und Familiennamen</u> 334
Reischauer, E.O. 528, 546
Renard, R. 180
Renaud, H. 461
Reychman, J. 289a
Reynolds, J.H. 35, 44
Ricchieri, G. 695
Richter, Eberhardt 666
Richter, Erich 251, 255, 256, 316, 519
Rigby, J.F. 233
Robinson, E. 451
Rodinson, M. 480
Roloff, H. 164
Romaji Fukyu Kai 533
Romaji Hirome Kai 538
Roman Alphabet Association of Japan, <u>see</u> Romaji Fukyu Kai
Roman Alphabet Propagating Society of Japan, <u>see</u> Romaji Hirome Kai
Romania. Oficiul de Stat pentru Standarde 242 a
Romano, D. 182a
Rondot, P. 409
Rosenthal, H. 299
Rost, R. 19
Rowland, P. 273
Royal Asiatic Society 401, 405
Royal Geographical Society 35, 716
Royal Institute of Thailand 672
Royal Society 221, 230
Ruska, J. 465
Ryba, B. 279

S., E.J. 20
Sacerdoțeanu, A. 185
Savina, V.I. 738
Ščerba, L.V. 229, 301, 306
Ščerbina, N. 345

Schade, W.   346
Scharschmidt, C.   564
Schleiermacher, A.A.E.   15
Schmid, A.   349
Schnorr von Carolsfeld, H.   66
Schrader, F.   697
Schramm, A.   22
Schramm, G.M.   438
Schröpfer, J.   32
Schubert, J.   410, 586
Schuchmann, M.   246
Schütz, E.   151
Schütz, F.   12, 575
Sedláček, K.   662, 670
Seitz, R.O.   556
Semičov, B.V.   670
Senaveratna, J.M.   724
Sengupta, B.   119
Serdjučenko, G.P.   418
Ševčik, A.   45
Ševoroškin, V.V.   191
Seybold, C.F.   447
Sharify, N.   144
Sharman, G.   626
Shaw, E.P.   72
Shaw, J.T.   327
Siew, Kee Yeh   82
Sigorskij, M.D.   522
Simon, W.   583, 595, 663
Sinor, D.   526
Sitadevi, A.   115
Smith, E.   451
Smith, H.D.U.   421
Smith, J.S.   296
Smolik, W.   257
Šnitke, G.V.   372
Society for the Development of the Persian Language   146
Somerville, J.C.   541
Sommer, F.E.   67, 68, 70, 113
Spain. Direccion general de archivos y bibliotecas   94
Spalding, C.S.   412, 414, 474
Stal'tman, V.E.   384
Stankievich, J.   367
Starostin, B.A.   386, 388
Starr Chester, K.   307
Steinhard, M.   194
Steinitz, W.   337
Stipčević, A.   83
Strong, R.M.   307
Subbiah, R.   572
Sunīti-Kumāra, Chattopādhyāya, <u>see</u> Chatterji, Suniti Kumar

Superanskaja, A.V. 51, 373, 732, 741
Supreme Commander for the Allied Powers 550
Susich, G. 318
Sweden. Sveriges Standardiseringskommission 259a
System Development Corporation 329a

Taeschner, F. 461, 466
Tam Wing Kuong, see T'an, Jung-Kuang
Tamaru, T. 548
T'an, Jung-Kuang 590, 610
Tanakadate, A. 535
Tanenbaum, R.D. 421
Täuber, H. 702, 703
Thomas, F.W. 639
Thompson, J.G. 13
Thomson, H.N. 312
Thys, E. 281, 288, 361, 470, 647
Tien, H.C. 622
Ting, Lee-Hsia Hsu 631
Tischner, J.K. 188, 244
Tjurin, S.A. 729, 735
Tolstoj, I.I. 385
Tomici, M. 277
Tomov, T.S. 175
Toponomastika i transkripcija 387, 741a
Trager, G.L. 215
Transkripcija geografičeskih nazvanij 733
Trautz, F.M. 563
Trevelyan, C.E. 397, 398, 399, 400
Treves, M. 184
Trnka, B. 286
Tronik, R. 79
Tsam Weing Guong, see T'an, Jung-Kuang
Tsukamoto, J.T. 557
Tucher, A.N. 682
Turkey. Maarif Vekâleti 91
Turover, G. Ja. 176

UFOD, see Union Française des Organismes de Documentation
Ubriatova, Ye. I. 377
Ulving, T. 617
Union Française des Organismes de Documentation 240
Union of Soviet Socialist Republics
   Central'nij Naučno-Issledovatel'skii Institut Geodezii, Aerosemki i Kartografii. Otdelenie transkripcii 742
   Komitet Standartov, Mer i Izmeritel'nyh Priborov 316a
   Ministerstvo Vnutrennih Del. 737
United Nations. Conference on the Standardization of Geographical Names 706, 710

United States
   Army. 500th Military Intelligence Group 673, 673a, 681
   Army Command Reconnaissance Activities, Pacific 615
   Army Language School 551, 611, 627
   Army Map Service. Geographic Names Branch 725
   Board on Geographic Names 711, 715, 721, 722
   Central Intelligence Agency 329
   Dept. of State. Office of the Geographer 711
   Government Printing Office 62
<u>Universal Jewish Encyclopedia</u> 430
Uspenskij, V.A. 328
Uustalu, E. 704

Văglenov, M. 530, 567
Vahros, I. 365
Vartapetjan, N.A. 153
Vasil'ev, V.P. 652
Vasil'kov, B.P. 53
Vatican. Biblioteca Vaticana, <u>see</u> Biblioteca Vaticana
Venn, H. 8
Vildé-Lot, I. 238
Virtosu, E. 242
Vissière, A. 641
Volney, C.F. 392, 394
Von Osterman, G.F. 46
Vorobeva-Desjatovskaja, M.I. 669

Wade, T. 576
Wagner, E. 92
Walsas, M. 161
Walter, A.J. 29
Walton, B. 1
Wang, Chin Chun 584, 593
Ward, P. 481
Ware, J.R. 589
Wechsler, B. 644
Weil, G. 512
Weinberg, W. 440
Weinreich, U. 199, 199a
Weissbach, F.H. 506
Werner, E.T.C. 594
Wharton, L.C. 40, 41, 43
Wheeler, G. 485
Wichner, F. 587
Wickens, G.M. 471
Wiener, L. 298
Wijk, N. van 360
Wiksel, J. 264
Wilkins, J. 2
Williams, M., <u>see</u> Monier-Williams, M.
Wilson, H.H. 106

Winkler, J. 351
Wood, M.M. 505
Wright, H.C. 78
Wylie, T. 667

Zafren, H.C. 441
Zajaczkowski, W. 416
Zavadovskij, Yu. N. 422
Zettersteen, K.V. 390
Zikmund, H. 192, 354
Žirkov, L. 292
Zlatoverhova, V.G. 677
Zottoli, A. 577

SUBJECT INDEX

Under the subheading Romanization are indexed: items dealing with the topic in general, international standards, and transcription or transliteration into English. The subheading Cyrillization implies transcription into Russian, unless specifically subdivided by language.

Afghanic, see Pushto
African languages
    Arabization 688
    Romanization 8, 682-687
Albanian
    Romanization 154, 155
Aljamiado, see Judeo-Arabic, Ladino
Alphabets 2, 5, 7, 13, 21-23, 28, 30, 31, 44, 46, 63
    Braille 109
    Phonetic 7, 9, 14, 15, 24, 25, 27, 51, 575
    Universal 2-7, 9-12, 14-18, 20, 23-25, 27, 64, 107
Altaic languages, see Mongolian, Tungus-Manchu, Turkish
American languages
    Romanization 689
Amharic script
    Cyrillization 422
    Romanization 86, 89, 497, 711
        German 66, 84, 87
Arabic script
    Chinese into A. 657, 658
    Cyrillization
        Bulgarian 493
        Place names 742
        Russian 418, 422
    Devanagari compared with 123
    Hebraization 460, 494
    Into Georgian 495
    Into Greek 419
    Judeo-Arabic 181, 182, 182a
    Romanization 67, 77, 86, 89-91, 98, 99, 126, 127, 135-140, 149, 391-394, 401, 403-405, 412, 414, 420, 451-486, 552, 747
        French 486-490
        German 66, 84, 87, 92, 492
        Italian 491
        Place names 451, 456, 458, 490, 711, 721, 722
        Portuguese 487
    Subject headings 482
Arabization
    African languages 688
    Chinese 657, 658
    French 183, 183a
    Indic languages 124
    Polish 289a
    Roman script 496
    Serbian 278, 278a, 278b
    Ukrainian 367

Aramaic, see Syriac
Armenian script
   Cyrillization 152
   Romanization 89, 150, 151, 325
      German 66, 84, 87
      Hungarian 153
Assamese
   Romanization 125
Assyrian
   Cyrillization 422
Avestan
   Romanization 84, 141

Bengali
   Romanization 126, 127
Berber
   Cyrillization 422
Bible 1, 13, 157, 425, 443, 444
Bibliographic work 65-94, 210, 211, 221, 259, 262, 265, 308, 311, 316, 320, 327, 355, 436
   See also Catalogs, Libraries
Botany 53, 220
Braille 109
Bulgarian
   Arabic into B. 493
   Czech into B. 282
   Greek into B. 170, 171
   Into Russian 274, 388
   Portuguese into B. 175
   Romanization 90, 206, 213, 221-226, 234, 273, 273a
      German 66, 84, 87, 253
      Place names 711
      Swedish 259
   Russian into B. 362
   Slovakian into B. 287
   Spanish into B. 174, 175
   Swedish into B. 203
   Ukrainian into B. 366
   White-Russian into B. 369
Burmese
   Cyrillization 676, 677
      Place names 744
   Non-Burmese scripts into B. 678
   Romanization 673, 674, 711
Cambodian
   Romanization 681, 681a, 711
Catalogs and cataloging 65-94
   Arabic 459, 482
   Chinese 618, 624, 629-631, 637
   Cyrillic 208-211, 315
   Hebrew 73, 79, 435, 439
   Indic languages 119

Catalogs and cataloging (cont.)
   Japanese 534, 542, 543, 545, 554, 557, 561
   Persian 144
   Rules 84-94
   Turkic languages 519, 520
   Turkish (Osmanli) 513, 514
   <u>See also</u> Bibliographic work, Libraries
Chemistry 552
Chinese
   Arabization 657, 658
   Cyrillization 418, 652-656
   English into C. 202
   Filing of entries 630, 637
   Hebrew into C. 448, 449
   Into Devanagari 639
   Into Korean 660, 661
   Into Tibetan 662-664
   Into Uigur 659
   Romanization 28, 29, 67, 77, 82, 414, 552, 575-638, 675
      Dutch 647, 648
      French 641, 642
      German 563, 645, 646
      Hungarian 650, 651
      Latin 577
      Place names 711, 725-727
      Polish 649
      Romanian 643, 644
      Spanish 640
Church Slavic, <u>see</u> Glagolitic script
Computers 121, 421, 441
Coptic
   Cyrillization 422
   Romanization 66, 84, 87, 89
Cyrillic script
   For non-Slavic languages 30, 63, 377, 386, 521, 522
      Romanization 229, 255, 269, 519, 520
   Japanese into C. 96
   Romanization 76, 77, 205-238
      Danish 257a
      Dutch 360, 361
      Finnish 365
      French 240, 240a
      German 60, 66, 84, 87, 243-257, 331-359
      Hungarian 267-271
      Polish 260-266, 364
      Portuguese 239, 239a
      Romanian 242, 242a
      Slovakian 363
      Spanish 331
      Swedish 258, 259, 259a
   <u>See also</u> Bulgarian, Macedonian, Russian, Serbian, Ukrainian, White-Russian

Cyrillization   29, 370-388, 418
    Amharic   422
    Arabic   418, 422, 491, 742
    Armenian   152
    Assyrian   422
    Berber   422
    Burmese   676, 677, 744
    Chinese   418, 652-656
    Coptic   422
    Czech   282-285, 388
    Danish   388
    Dutch   388
    English   200-201a, 355, 378, 388, 740, 741
    Finnish   388
    French   355, 388
    Georgian   499, 500
    German   188-192, 388, 739
    Greek   170, 171
    Haussa   422
    Hebrew   422
    Hindi   418
    Hungarian   388
    Italian   388
    Japanese   418, 566, 567
    Korean   418, 530
    Mongolian   418
    Norwegian   388
    Persian   418, 738
    Place names   729-744
    Polish   289, 388
    Portuguese   175, 388
    Pushto   418
    Romanian   388
    Serbian   388
    Slovakian   287, 388
    Spanish   174-176, 388
    Swedish   203, 388
    Syriac   422
    Tibetan   669, 670
    Turkic languages in USSR   28, 229, 519-522
    Turkish (Osmanli)   515
    Ugaritic   422
    Vietnamese   680
Czech   32, 213, 234, 279
    Cyrillic into C.   212, 215
    Cyrillization
        Bulgarian   282
        Russian   283-285, 388
    Into Dutch   281
    Into Romanian   280
    Oriental scripts into C.   414a

124

Danish
   Cyrillic into D. 257a
   Cyrillization 388
   Russian into D. 361a
Devanagari script (and its modifications)
   Chinese into D. 639
   Romanization 4, 6, 13, 65, 66, 70, 81, 82, 84-87, 97-123, 125-128, 132-134, 395-405, 408-411, 414, 418, 569-574, 711, 724
Diacritical marks 31, 32
Dravidian languages
   Romanization 13, 569-574
Dutch
   Chinese into D. 647, 648
   Cyrillization 388

Egyptian
   Into Greek 419
English
   Cyrillization 200-201a, 355, 378, 388
      Place names 740, 741
   Into Chinese 202

Faeroese 711
Filing of Chinese entries 630, 637
Finnish
   Cyrillic into F. 365
   Cyrillization 388
French
   Arabic into F. 486-488
   Arabization 183, 183a
   Chinese into F. 641, 642
   Cyrillic into F. 240
   Cyrillization 355, 388
   Place names into F. 696
Fula
   Romanization 683

Gaelic
   Romanization 186, 187
Geography, see Place names
Geometry 476
Georgian script
   Arabic into G. 495
   Cyrillization 499, 500
   In Greek MSS. 172
   Romanization 325
      German 84, 87
      Hungarian 498
German
   Arabic into G. 66, 84, 87, 92, 492
   Bulgarian into G. 66, 84, 87, 253
   Chinese into G. 563, 645, 646

German (cont.)
   Cyrillic into G. 60, 66, 84, 242-257, 331-339
   Cyrillization 188-192, 388
      Place names 739
   Hebraization 193-195
   Hebrew into G. 66, 84, 87, 427
   Hindi into G. 66, 84, 87, 129
   Japanese into G. 563-566, 646
   Malayalam into G. 66, 84, 87
   Pahlavi into G. 84
   Persian into G. 66, 84, 87, 92, 143
   Place names into G. 708, 709, 717-720
   Pushto into G. 66, 84
   Romanian into G. 87
   Russian into G. 66, 84, 87, 253, 331-339
      Place names 334, 351, 717-720
   Sanskrit into G. 66, 84, 87
   Script 29
   Serbian into G. 84, 87, 253
   Syriac into G. 66, 84, 87
   Turkish into G. 66, 84, 87, 92, 513
   Ukrainian into G. 87, 253
   White-Russian into G. 253
Glagolitic script 234
   Romanization 226, 272
      German 84, 87
Greek script
   Cyrillization, Bulgarian 170, 171
   Georgian script in Greek MSS. 172
   Oriental scripts into G. 390, 419
   Romanization 62, 86, 88-90, 107, 156-169
      German 84, 87, 169
      Place names 711, 714
      Spanish 167, 168
Gujarati
   Romanization 128
Gurmukhi script
   Romanization 134
Gypsy languages
   Romanization 690

Hamito-Semitic languages (in general)
   Cyrillization 422
   Into Greek 419
   Romanization 420-421
Haussa
   Cyrillization 422
Hebraization
   Arabic 428, 494
   German 193-195
   Italian 184
   Non-Hebrew scripts into H. 450, 450a

Hebrew script
    Catalogs 73, 79, 435, 439
    Cyrillization 422
    Into Chinese 448, 449
    Into Greek 419, 443, 444
    Into Lithuanian 445
    Into Polish 446
    Romanization 62, 65, 86, 89, 90, 325, 405, 420, 423-442, 748
        By computer 421, 441
        German 66, 84, 87, 427
        Place names 711
    See also Judeo-Arabic, Ladino, Yiddish
Hindi
    Cyrillization 418
    Romanization 13, 115, 130
        German 66, 84, 87, 129
Hungarian 501
    Armenian into H. 153
    Chinese into H. 650, 651
    Cyrillic into H. 267-271
    Cyrillization 388
    Georgian into H. 498
    Macedonian into H. 275
Hunnic-Magyarian script 501
Huzvareš, see Pahlavi

Icelandic 711
Indexes 80
Indo-Aryan languages (in general)
    Romanization 4, 6, 81, 97-153, 391-416
        Place names 711-713
International Organization for Standardization (ISO) 49, 52, 54, 57,
    164, 229, 238, 266, 322, 323, 433, 436, 478, 481
Italian
    Arabic into I. 491
    Cyrillization 388
    Hebraization 184
    Into Serbian 276

Japanese script
    Cyrillization
        Bulgarian 567
        Russian 418, 566
    Non-Japanese scripts into J. 568
    Romanization 22, 77, 533-566, 602, 638, 746, 749
        German 563-566, 646
        Place names 711
Judeo-Arabic 178, 181, 182, 182a
    Hebrew and J. 447

Kannada
    Romanization 13, 122, 569

127

Khmer, see Cambodian
Korean script
    Chinese into K. 660, 661
    Cyrillization
        Bulgarian 530
        Russian 418
    Non-Korean scripts into K. 532
    Romanization 77, 527-529
        Place names 711, 723
Kurdish
    Romanization 139, 140

Ladino 177-180
Laotian
    Romanization 673a, 711
Lappish 711
Latin 156-158, 279
    Chinese into L. 577
    Into Greek 419
    Into Romanian 173
Latinization 28, 42
    Chinese, *see* Chinese: Romanization
    Japanese, *see* Japanese: Romanization
    Russian 22, 29, 290-294, 518
    Turkic languages in USSR 516-518
    Turkish (Osmanli) 22, 29, 91, 502-508
Latvian
    Lithuanian into L. 204
Libraries 65-83, 122, 267, 439, 479, 514, 637
    See also Bibliographic work, Catalogs
Linguistics 59, 608
Lithuanian
    Hebrew into L. 445
    Into Latvian 204
Lord's Prayer 19, 23, 424, 689

Macedonian
    Cataloging 83
    Romanization 222-226, 234, 236, 261
        Hungarian 275
        Place names 711
        Swedish 259
Malayalam
    Romanization 13, 82, 414, 573
        German 66, 84, 87
Maldivian script
    Romanization 711
Manchu script
    Romanization 525, 526
Maps, *see* Place names
Marathi
    Romanization 131

MARC system   31
Mathematics   476
Maya
   Romanization   689
Mongolian script
   Cyrillization   418
   Into Chinese   524
   Latinization   518, 523
   Romanization   711

Negro languages, see African languages
Nepali
   Romanization 711
Non-Slavic languages, Cyrillic script used by   30, 63, 377, 386, 521, 522
   Romanization   229, 255, 269, 519, 520
Norwegian
   Cyrillization   388

Oriental languages (in general)
   Cataloging   81, 82
   Cyrillization   417, 418
   Into Greek   390, 419
   Romanization   10, 109, 391-416
Oriya
   Romanization   132, 133
Osmanli, see Turkish (Osmanli)

Pahlavi
   Romanization   142
Panjabi
   Romanization   134
Pashtu, see Pushto
Persian
   Cyrillization   418
     Place names   738
   Romanization   89, 144-147, 391-394
     German   66, 84, 87, 92, 143
     Place names   711, 715, 721
Place names
   Cyrillization   729-737
     From Arabic   742
     From Burmese   744
     From English   740, 741
     From German   739
     From Persian   738
     From Turkic languages   743
   Romanization   691-711
     From Arabic   490, 721, 722
     From Chinese   725-727
     From Greek   714
     From Indic languages   712, 713
     From Korean   723

Place names
    Romanization (cont.)
        From Persian 715, 721
        From Russian 716-720
        From Singhalese 724
        From Tibetan 728
        Into English 35, 44, 691-693, 711
        Into French 490, 696
        Into German 708, 709
        Into Romanian 707
    Transcription into Chinese 745
Polish 213, 234
    Arabization 289a
    Chinese into P. 649
    Cyrillic into P. 260-266, 364
    Cyrillization 289, 388
    Hebrew into P. 446
    Into Dutch 288
    Oriental scripts into P. 415, 416
Portuguese
    Arabic into P. 485
    Cyrillic into P. 239, 239a
    Cyrillization 388
    Into Bulgarian 175
Prakrit
    Romanization 99, 100
Pushto
    Cyrillization 418
    Romanization 149, 711
        German 66, 84

Reform of national scripts, <u>see</u> Latinization
Re-transliteration 80, 95, 96, 344, 355
Romanian
    Chinese into R. 643, 644
    Cyrillic into R. 242a
    Cyrillization 388
    Place names into R. 707
    Romanization of R. written in Cyrillic script 88, 226
        German 87
        Into modern Romanian 185, 241
Russian
    Into Bulgarian 362
    Latinization 22, 29, 290-294, 518
    Romanization 62, 65, 67, 90, 206, 213, 221-226, 234-236, 295-330
        Danish 361a
        Dutch 360, 361
        Finnish 365
        French 240
        German 66, 84, 87, 253, 331-359
        Hungarian 267-271

Russian
   Romanization (cont.)
      Place names 306, 313, 711, 716
         German 334, 357, 717-720
      Polish 260, 364
      Portuguese 239
      Slovakian 363
      Spanish 331
      Swedish 258, 259
   See also Cyrillic script

Sanskrit
   Arabization 101
   Into Chinese 102, 103
   Romanization 65, 85, 86, 97-100, 113
      German 66, 84, 87
Scripts 1-33
   See also under individual scripts
Semitic languages (in general)
   Cyrillization 422
   Into Greek 419
   Romanization 10, 15, 65, 420-421
Serbian
   Arabization 278, 278a, 278b
   Cataloging 83
   Into Russian 388
   Italian into S. 276
   Romanization 90, 213, 221-226, 234-236, 261
      German 84, 87, 253
      Place names 711
      Romanian 277
      Swedish 259
Siamese, see Thai
Sindhi in Arabic script
   Romanization 135
Sinhalese
   Romanization 135a
      Place names 724
Slavic languages (in general)
   Romanization 15, 23, 32, 62, 66, 76, 77, 86, 88-90, 205-271
   See also Cyrillic script
Slovakian
   Cyrillic into S. 363
   Cyrillization
      Bulgarian 287
      Russian 388
Slovenian 234
Spanish
   Chinese into S. 640
   Cyrillization
      Bulgarian 174, 175
      Russian 176, 388

Spanish (cont.)
    Non-Roman scripts into S. 94
    See also Judeo-Arabic, Ladino
Standardization, see International Organization for Standardization
Sudano-Guinean languages
    Romanization 685-687
Swedish
    Cyrillic into S. 258, 259, 259a
    Cyrillization
        Bulgarian 203
        Russian 388
Syriac
    Cyrillization 422
    Romanization 86, 89, 422, 429
        By computer 421
        German 66, 84, 87

Tamil script
    Romanization 13, 82, 115, 570-572
        Place names 724
Taxonomic nomenclature 53, 158, 159, 220, 232, 233, 739
Telegrams 324, 682
Telugu script
    Romanization 13, 574
Thai script
    Romanization 671-675, 711
Tibetan script
    Chinese into T. 662-664
    Cyrillization 669-670
    Romanization 666-668
        Place names 728
Turkic languages in the U.S.S.R.
    Cyrillization 28, 229, 519-522
        Place names 743
    Latinization 516-518
    Romanization 519, 520
Turkish (Osmanli)
    Cyrillization 515
    Latinization 22, 29, 91, 502-508
    Romanization 89, 91, 392-394, 509-514
        German 66, 84, 87, 92, 513
Typewriting 314, 636

Ugaritic
    Cyrillization 422
    Romanization by computer 421
Uigur script
    Chinese into U. 659
Ukrainian
    Arabization 367
    Into Bulgarian 366

Ukrainian (cont.)
   Romanization 90, 222-226, 234-236
      German 87, 253
      Place names 711
      Polish 261
      Swedish 259, 259a
Universal alphabets 2-7, 9-12, 14-18, 20, 23-25, 27, 64, 107
Uralian languages, <u>see</u> Finnish, Hungarian
Urdu
   Romanization 136-138, 711

Vietnamese
   Cyrillization 680
   Romanization 679
      Place names 710

White-Russian
   Into Bulgarian 369
   Romanization 90, 222-226, 234-236
      German 253
      Hungarian 368
      Polish 261
      Swedish 259

Yiddish
   Romanization 90, 196-199a, 325
     By computer 421
   <u>See also</u> Hebrew

Zend, see Avestan
Zoology 158, 159